Thou sayest that I am a king. To this end was I born, and for this cause came I into the world, that I should bear witness unto the truth. JOHN 18:37

FOR THIS CAUSE

The Third of Three Books of Trinity Sermons

BY PASTORS OF
THE EVANGELICAL LUTHERAN CHURCH

Augsburg Publishing House · Minneapolis

Contents

TWENTY-SECOND SUNDAY AFTER TRINITY

TWENTY-THIRD SUNDAY AFTER TRINITY

TWENTY-SIXTH SUNDAY AFTER TRINITY

EIGHTEENTH SUNDAY AFTER TRINITY

But when the Pharisees had heard that he had put the Sadducees to silence, they were gathered together. Then one of them, which was a lawyer, asked him a question, tempting him, and saying, Master, which is the great commandment in the law? Jesus said unto him, Thou shalt love the Lord thy God with all thy heart, and with all thy soul, and with all thy mind. This is the first and great commandment. And the second is like unto it, Thou shalt love thy neighbor as thyself. On these two commandments hang all the law and the prophets.

While the Pharisees were gathered together, Jesus asked them, saying, What think ye of Christ? whose son is he? They say unto him, The son of David. He saith unto them, How then doth David in spirit call him Lord, saying, The Lord said unto my Lord, Sit thou on my right hand, till I make thine enemies thy footstool? If David then call him Lord, how is he his son? And no man was able to answer him a word, neither durst any man from that day forth ask him any more questions.

MATTHEW 22:34-46

Chapter One

Questions Without Quest

A QUESTION is not always a quest for truth. A questioner is not always actuated by a desire to gain information. This is especially true of many who raise questions regarding the teachings of Holy Writ. Some ask questions of Christian believers not for the purpose of receiving spiritual enlightenment, but to try to catch those questioned in contradictions, hoping to show up alleged fallacies of the teachings of Christianity.

Others who ask questions devoid of quest for truth do so because they hope by the answers received to confute the doctrinal position of those to whom their questions are addressed, and thus to establish their own preconceived concepts.

This was the case with the Pharisees who on the occasion told of in our text asked Jesus, "Which is the great commandment of the law?" They did not ask because they hoped to receive an authoritative answer, one that would be the final pronouncement in the matter. They themselves were not agreed as to which of the law's commandments ought to be given priority. Among the interpreters of the law in those days some were inclined to give preference to the laws demanding sacrifice; others would place the law regarding the Sabbath as the foremost commandment. All, however, were of one mind as to making a distinction between the so-called great commandments and those of minor importance. To the commandments regarded as great they would give meticulous observance in an outward way; those looked upon as secondary they felt at liberty to disregard, more or less.

It is not clear just what the Pharisees hoped to accomplish by their question put to Jesus. It is possible that they hoped by His answer to show that this would-be rabbi, this upstart from Galilee, was wholly ignorant of the theologic thought of the day, and hence one to be wholly ignored as an interpreter of the divine law. It is also possible that they, uneasily feeling that this strange Nazarene had a conception of the law entirely at variance with their own, wanted to sound Him out in this matter. In the latter case they did indeed ask to gain information of a sort, but their question was, even so, no quest for truth, for they most assuredly did not mean to adopt His view. Superciliously they were too much enamored with their

own learning and insight to profit by the teachings of this "outsider."

Being the Divine One, Jesus knew the hearts of
His questioners; He knew that they did not ask
to be guided into the truth. He, nevertheless, did
not answer the fool after his folly, as mere men
are too often tempted to do. He gave them a
serious answer, one that dealt directly with the
matter involved in the question.

Why did He do so? Doubtless because He knew
as no one else the power of the Word. He knew
that whereas no shell is harder to penetrate than
the shell with which self-complacency encases
the heart; nevertheless, no other force than God's
own Word can pierce that hard shell.

The parallel passage in Mark 12 throws light
on the purpose of the answer of Jesus. That passage gives us reason for believing that the particular spokesman for the Pharisaic group on this
occasion was in his heart more attracted toward
the Galilean rabbi than were most of his asso-
ciates, perhaps more deeply than he himself was
aware of. He was among those Pharisees who perceived that Jesus had spoken well in answering
the catch question of the Sadducees. After Jesus
had answered the question of his own group he
gave a thoughtful comment. Whereupon Jesus
said to him, "Thou art not far from the kingdom
of God."

Very likely Jesus answered the question in so

serious a manner out of consideration for the quest which He discerned in the depth of the spokesman's heart. In regard to this far-seeing soul-care of the Lord, someone has said, "Even when surrounded by hostile tempters and carping critics Christ kept the eye of His seeking love undimmed, thus divining even the most hidden response in the hearts of men whose faces remained hard and closed."

The answer of Jesus quietly rebukes the Pharisees' faulty interpretation of the law. It shows that even as God is one, so His law is one; that he who stumbles in one point is become guilty of all the commandments. This it does by pointing out that love is the great commandment of the law, not because of any supposed inferiority of the other commandments, but because love is the very chain linking the entire law together into one inseparable whole. "On these two commandments," the one enjoining love to God and its practical application, love to one's neighbor—"the whole law hangeth."

Having thus effectively and convincingly answered their question, which, as far as the group was concerned, was indeed a question without quest for truth, Jesus in turn directs a question to them: How could it be that the Messiah, who according to Scripture and their own assertion was the Son of David, was also by David himself called his Lord? This question of Jesus had as its

purpose to put His questioners into a real quest
for truth. Their question had been devoid of this
quest. It was, in the first place, based on a wrong
interpretation of the law and, in the next place,
it was actuated by a woeful want of love. Thus
their very question was a breaking of the law,
regarding the observance of which they professed
such great zeal.

If they would cease busying themselves with
such barren questions as to which of the many
detailed commandments of the law should be
placed first and, incidentally, which might with
comparative impunity be slighted, and instead
turn to a real search of the Scriptures, they would
be in a real quest for truth. Then they would in
their searchings find the Christ who is the very
end of the law unto righteousness. Then, in place
of opposing Him when He came unto them, they
would receive Him as at the same time the Son
of man and his Lord.

In our day many ask questions not inspired
by any quest for truth. They seize upon details of
scriptural revelation which cannot be answered
so long as the questioner rejects or disregards the
very center of that revelation. Or, they follow in
the footsteps of the Pharisees by dividing the law
of God into great and small commandments and
by classifying transgressions of the law into sins
and peccadilloes—of which the former commonly
be few and the latter many.

EIGHTEENTH SUNDAY AFTER TRINITY

And Jesus walked in the temple in Solomon's porch. Then came the Jews around about him, and said unto him, How long dost thou make us to doubt? If thou be the Christ, tell us plainly. Jesus answered them, I told you, and ye believed not: the works that I do in my Father's name, they bear witness of me. But ye believe not, because ye are not of my sheep, as I said unto you. My sheep hear my voice, and I know them, and they follow me: And I give unto them eternal life; and they shall never perish, neither shall any man pluck them out of my hand. My Father, which gave them me, is greater than all; and no man is able to pluck them out of my Father's hand. I and my Father are one. Then the Jews took up stones again to stone him. Jesus answered them, Many good works have I shewed you from my Father; for which of those works do ye stone me? The Jews answered him, saying, For a good work we stone thee not; but for blasphemy; and because that thou, being a man, makest thyself God. Jesus answered them, Is it not written in your law, I said, Ye are gods? If he called them gods, unto whom the word of God came, and the scripture cannot be broken; say ye of him, whom the Father hath sanctified, and sent into the world, Thou blasphemest; because I said, I am the Son of God? If I do not the works of my Father, believe me not. But if I do, though ye believe not me, believe the works: that ye may know, and believe, that the Father is in me, and I in him.

JOHN 10:23-38

Chapter Two

The Gift of Eternal Life

WE ARE living in challenging times. The very air we breathe is vibrant with change and the portents of change. Customs and traditions which have held sway for many centuries are being destroyed and relegated into the background. Thoughtful men everywhere nourish fearful apprehension as to what the future may hold in store for mankind.

The signs of spiritual disintegration and moral decay are everywhere about us. Everywhere men are held in the grip of haunting, terrifying fear. Atomic energy speaks mightily concerning the possibility of the destruction of civilization. John R. Mott tells us we are facing one of the most tragic and fateful moments in all history. Albert Schweitzer said some years ago, "It is clear now to everyone that the suicide of civilization is in progress." Many of the things man has trusted, believed in, and leaned upon have fallen into a heap of ruins at his very feet.

The seriousness of our times only adds lustre and significance to the words of Christ, "I give unto them eternal life. They shall never perish, and no one shall snatch them out of my hand." However dark the age in which man has lived, his faith in the promises of God has brought him hope, courage, and inspiration. In spite of physical hardship and immeasurable suffering, the apostle Paul carried on with joy. His triumphant faith in Christ enabled him to say, "Whether I live or die I am the Lord's." Luther expresses that faith in the hymn:

> And should they, in the strife,
> Take kindred, goods, and life,
> We freely let them go,
> They profit not the foe;
> With us remains the kingdom.

The dominant note in our text is eternal life. This message of hope was spoken by our Lord during one of the annual celebrations of the feast of dedication. This festival was in commemoration of the cleansing of the Temple which had been pilfered and desecrated by Antiochus Epiphanes. After the enemies of the Jews were driven from Jerusalem and the Temple, a feast of dedication was proclaimed by Judas Maccabeus in the year 167 B.C. The people of Palestine recognized this event during the middle of December, and the festival lasted for eight days.

Jesus was in Jerusalem during the time of this feast. He makes use of this opportunity to testify once more that He is the Son of God. One day He appears in the Temple on Solomon's porch. It was on the east side of the Temple court, and faced the valley of Kidron. Nebuchadnezzar had destroyed the Temple, and this little portico under which Jesus was walking on this occasion was the only section which remained. Immediately the Jews took advantage of the situation to ask Him questions concerning His person, "How long will you keep us in suspense? If you are the Christ, tell us plainly."

They are skeptical concerning His Messiahship, and were even ready and willing to put Him to death. Their intention to destroy Him is clearly revealed when a little later they took up stones to destroy Him. In response to their question Jesus said, "I told you, and ye believed not: the works that I do in my Father's name, these bear witness of me." Time and again He testified concerning Himself as the promised Savior. His words and deeds are living evidences attesting His deity.

It is true that He had not revealed Himself to all as clearly as He had to the woman of Samaria at Sychar, to whom He said, "I that speak unto thee am he," or to the man born blind, "It is he that talketh with thee." The testimony support-

ing His Messiahship had been so impressive, however, that a man like Nicodemus came to Him one
night and said, "We know that thou art a teacher
come from God, for no man can do these miracles
that thou doest, except God be with him."

To this group of unbelieving Jews our Lord
says, "I and my Father are one." This statement
clearly supports His sonship with God. What
more could He add to what He had already said?
He had repeatedly reminded them of His works
and miracles. They should have remembered how
He had restored sight to the blind, speech to the
mute; how He had cured the sick, helped the
suffering, and strengthened the discouraged. His
purpose in declaring His divinity was to impress
upon them the supreme importance of establish-
ing their citizenship in His kingdom which shall
endure when all other kingdoms crumble to dust.

Definitely and distinctly He had revealed His
identity. He was the Light of the world, the Bread
of life. In an effort to make them understand His
position in God's economy of grace, He said to
them, "If I do not the works of my Father, believe me not." Yet the Jews, blinded by ignorance,
pride, prejudice, and false notions concerning His
Messiahship, had closed their hearts to His saving
message. The trouble with the Jews themselves
was that they would not believe.

Unbelief is not something confined to the time
and contemporaries of Christ. It is an ever-present

evil much in evidence in the world today. Some recent dictators thought Christ was unessential. They did not believe in the authenticity of Christianity, or in saints and apostles. They did not believe in the divine origin of the Bible, in salvation by supernatural means, or in the doctrine of immortality. They did not realize that to miss Christ is to miss life's highest good, life's richest blessings, and the gift of eternal salvation.

All men are asking, "Is human life a journey to oblivion or a prelude to eternity? Is it an ascent to God or a descent to dust?" Omar Khayyam, the Persian philosopher and poet of the eighth century, A.D., rejected the Christian doctrines and tried to solve the riddle of life without the aid of divine revelation. Desperately he labored to discover the meaning of life and man's ultimate destiny. The task was, of course, impossible, even for one with his penetrating mind. It is too great for anyone who seeks to understand and explain life without the guiding light radiating from the Son of God. Despairing in his search for the purpose of life, Khayyam said, "Some little talk a while of me and thee—and then no more of thee and me."

We have no dearth of skeptics and unbelievers. Macbeth says, "Life is a tale, told by an idiot." "Death is better," says Heine. "Life is a jest," cries the cynic. Solomon says, "Vanity of vanities." The Jews said concerning Christ, "For a good work we stone thee not; but for blasphemy." How often our hearts are bowed with grief as we read that they would not believe.

On a previous occasion in Jerusalem Jesus endeavored to influence the unbelieving Jews. How beautifully He describes Himself as the Good Shepherd. Tenderly and compassionately He speaks of His love and care for the sheep. Regardless of His efforts to win them to His heart of love, the unbelievers would not hearken unto His voice

What great happiness and joy come to those who know and love the Shepherd! Not only do they discern His voice amid the clamor of other voices, but they are ever ready and willing to follow. "My sheep hear my voice, and I know them, and they follow me." What a marvelous thing to be known and loved of the Son of God! Our Lord says of His sheep, "I give unto them eternal life; and they shall never perish, neither shall any man pluck them out of my hand. My Father, which gave them me, is greater than all; and no man is able to pluck them out of my Father's hand. I and my Father are one."

No greater gift can come to anyone than the gift of eternal life. It is a free, unmerited gift to all mankind. It cannot be earned. It is received through faith in the Son of God. Eternal Life! Somehow those words invade our ears and we see visions and dream dreams. They speak to us of the New Jerusalem: "And the city had no need of the sun, neither of the moon, to shine in it: for the glory of God did lighten it, and the Lamb is the light thereof."

This can be our possession. "He that believeth and is baptized shall be saved." What marvelous words of assurance! "This is my Father's will, that of all which he hath given me I should lose nothing, but should raise it up again the last day." Possessing the great gift of salvation, we gladly hear His Word, partake of His Sacraments, and dedicate ourselves to unselfish Christian service.

Martineau once said, "We do not believe in immortality because we can prove it; but we try to prove it because we cannot help believing it." It is a universal longing. Man's spirit does not decline with the years. His brow may be adorned with the snow of many years, his footsteps may falter, his strength of body may ebb, but his hopes and yearnings are never fully reached in this life. Life at best here on earth is incomplete and fragmentary. Phillips Brooks said, "Death is not the end of life; death is only an incident in the course of life." Winfred Rhoades was right when he said, "The Resurrection sings humanity's dream of fulfillment."

The promise of Christ to all His followers is the gift of everlasting salvation. "God so loved the world, that he gave his only begotten Son, that whosoever believeth in him should not perish, but have everlasting life." No power in the world can crush those who are in Christ. God and His Son are pledged to keep them, and they shall never perish. Have faith. The greatest need of our sin-ridden, shaken, unbelieving, war-torn world is to return to faith in Christ. What great blessings would come if we would but "live under Him in His kingdom and serve Him in everlasting righteousness, innocence, and blessedness."

The hope of the world is not to be found in pursuit of the philosophies of men, but a glorious discovery of the teachings of Christ; not in clever doubting, but in triumphant believing; not in selfish gain, but in unselfish service. Courageously we can face the future with Him who said, "I give unto them eternal life." "Blessed be the God and Father of our Lord Jesus Christ, which according to his abundant mercy hath begotten us again unto a lively hope by the resurrection of Jesus Christ from the dead."

AMEN

EIGHTEENTH SUNDAY AFTER TRINITY

And when he was gone forth into the way, there came one running, and kneeled to him, and asked him, Good Master, what shall I do that I may inherit eternal life? And Jesus said unto him, Why callest thou me good? there is none good but one, that is, God. Thou knowest the commandments, Do not commit adultery, Do not kill, Do not steal, Do not bear false witness, Defraud not, Honour thy father and mother. And he answered and said unto him, Master, all these have I observed from my youth. Then Jesus beholding him loved him, and said unto him, One thing thou lackest: go thy way, sell whatsoever thou hast, and give to the poor, and thou shalt have treasure in heaven: and come, take up the cross, and follow me. And he was sad at that saying, and went away grieved: for he had great possessions.

And Jesus looked round about, and saith unto his disciples, How hardly shall they that have riches enter into the kingdom of God! And the disciples were astonished at his words. But Jesus answereth again, and saith unto them, Children, how hard is it for them that trust in riches to enter into the kingdom of God! It is easier for a camel to go through the eye of a needle, than for a rich man to enter into the kingdom of God. And they were astonished out of measure, saying among themselves, Who then can be saved? And Jesus looking upon them saith, With men it is impossible, but not with God: for with God all things are possible.

MARK 10:17-27

Chapter Three

Almost a Disciple

ONE day, just after mail call on our South Sea
island, a young man came into my tent and
said, "Padre, look what my mother sent me." He
held up a Bible. "I wonder why she sent it. Maybe she's worried that I might be drinking too
much." I asked him if he had ever read the Bible,
and he said he had not. "Where should I start?"
I suggested he read the Gospel according to St.
John and invited him to come back at his con-
venience and discuss what he had read. I didn't
see him for two weeks.

Then one evening he invited me to his tent. I
asked if he had done any reading in his new Bible.
Oh, yes—all four of the gospels and several of the
epistles. He explained he had been reading nothing else and pointed out his shelf of books that he
had built into a sea chest that could be opened
and closed conveniently—books on philosophy,
English, history, and sociology. This was some-

thing different from the books one ordinarily saw in the barracks.

"Have you discovered why your mother sent you this Bible?"

"Well, no, but there's something I want to ask you."

He handed me a list of twenty-five or thirty Bible passages and said, "Explain these." We sat down, and tried to see what these passages from God's Word could mean. Some of the verses were difficult, and I admitted my lack of complete understanding. Later in the conversation, I asked whether he had discovered some of the verses that are so clear and definite and unmistakable when they speak about our sin and man's helplessness in spiritual matters, as well as some of the verses that tell us of God's grace and mercy and the coming of Jesus Christ to save sinners. He admitted he had read some of those passages, but added that he was still concerned about some of the things he could not understand. But he said he was going to keep reading

A few days later he was transferred to a unit on another island. Two months went by. Then, on a chance trip to visit a chaplain who had just come from the States, I was hailed by a familiar voice as I drove my borrowed jeep along a jungle trail. It was the young lieutenant. "Hello, Padre! I've found the philosophy of life I've been looking for." He stepped into his tent, picked up a thin book from his shelf, and came back to the jeep. "Omar Khayyam has the answer." He read a stanza from *The Rubaiyat:*

Yesterday *This* Day's Madness did prepare;
Tomorrow's Silence, Triumph, or Despair:
Drink! for you know not whence you came, nor why:
Drink! for you know not why you go, nor where.

One day, a certain lawyer stood up, and tempted Jesus, saying, "Master, what shall I do to inherit eternal life?" The spirit in which he asked the question indicates that he did not want to hear the truth. But Jesus answered him, telling him of the demands of the law and leading him beyond the law to the gospel of love. He was almost a disciple.

When Paul the apostle was taken before Governor Felix and allowed to speak of the faith in Christ, Paul reasoned about righteousness, temperance, and the judgment to come. Felix became alarmed and said, "Go away for the present; when I have an opportunity I will summon you." Almost a disciple.

When Paul appeared before King Agrippa, Paul spoke of his former hatred of Christ, then described his conversion on the Damascus road. He told how the Lord had appointed him as an apostle to the Gentiles, to open their eyes, and to turn them from darkness to light, and from the power of Satan unto God, that they may receive forgiveness of sins and sonship with God. Agrippa was stirred by Paul's words, and said to him, "Almost thou persuadest me to be a Christian." Almost a disciple.

The old gospel song impresses upon our hearts that tragic condition:

"Almost persuaded," now to believe;
"Almost persuaded" Christ to receive;
Seems now some soul to say, "Go, Spirit, go Thy way,
Some more convenient day on Thee I'll call."

"Almost persuaded," come, come today;
"Almost persuaded," turn not away;
Jesus invites you here, angels are lingering near,
Prayers rise from hearts so dear: O wanderer, come.
                                        PHILIP P. BLISS

Down through the centuries, countless thousands have asked the question, "What shall I do that I may inherit eternal life?" Many of them, with the three thousand convicted sinners of the day of Pentecost, have heard the answer of the gospel, "Repent, and be baptized every one of you in the name of Jesus Christ for the remission of sins." Known only to God are those who have sincerely repented and found grace and peace in Him. Known only to God are those who have rejected the gospel, rejected His Word, not because they could not understand and reason out every truth, but because there are so many things they can understand. The Bible is so understandable when it touches my sin.

Matthew, Mark, and Luke all describe the visit

of the young man to Jesus; the one who came running, and kneeled down before Him and asked, "Good Master, what shall I do that I may inherit eternal life?" He was sincere in his question. He knew there was something he needed. Jesus said, "Thou knowest the commandments, Do not commit adultery, Do not kill, Do not steal, Do not bear false witness, Defraud not, Honor thy father and mother." He answered, "Master, all these have I observed from my youth." His answer revealed the fact that he had no real knowledge of the law. He outwardly obeyed the law, but he was ignorant of the spirit of the law.

Sometimes you feel that you can make that same claim, "All these things have I observed from my youth." Like that young man, however, we need to learn from Jesus that the law demands my whole being, heart, and soul, and mind, and body. "Do not commit adultery," be pure in heart. Keep your heart from the defilement of carnal desires. Chastity in the sight of men is not enough. Freedom from outward immorality is not enough. Your heart must be pure in the sight of God.

"Do not kill," love your fellow men, so that you do not injure them by thought, word, or deed. Love them so that you do good to them that hate you, bless them that curse you, pray for them that despitefully use you.

"Do not steal," do not take or destroy your

neighbor's property. Grant unto every man his rights. Suffer personal wrong rather than profit at the expense of another. "Do not bear false witness." Not only must you observe the sanctity of an oath before a court of justice, but your daily life must bear witness of a love in deed and truth. Your love must express itself in words, so that you speak ill of no one. "Bless them that persecute you; bless, and curse not." "Honor thy father and thy mother." Show in your everyday life the Christian virtues of a child, of a father or mother, of husband or wife, of brother or sister, of employer or employee, of teacher or pupil, in other words, all the duties of family, church, and state.

"This do, and thou shalt live," said Jesus to the lawyer who asked Him what he should do to inherit eternal life. To you and to me Jesus says the same, "This do, and thou shalt live." Jesus enumerates every requirement. Every one is impossible!

Why? Because there is one thing thou lackest. To that rich young man, to the lawyer, the King Agrippa, the governor of Judea, that young navy lieutenant, to every unrepentant sinner today comes that same word of Jesus, "One thing thou lackest." The thing each one lacks begins with this discovery—the realization that all his work-righteousness is in vain, that what he needs is a complete inward change. "Ye must be born again."

Jesus told the young man exactly what was

involved in the change. "One thing thou lackest: go thy way, sell whatsoever thou hast, and give to the poor, and thou shalt have treasure in heaven: and come, take up the cross, and follow me." Jesus laid His finger on the great sin in his heart, his love of earthly possessions. With that barrier remaining between him and Jesus, he could not follow Him and inherit eternal life. An inner change, beginning with true repentance for his sin in placing an idol—his material possessions—above the true God, was his need.

Are we to believe that this was an isolated case? Has it never happened since? Does it not happen today that men outwardly conform to religious respectability, but inwardly worship an idol? The words of Jesus ring out, "No man can serve two masters! Ye cannot serve God and mammon!"

Jesus invited the young man to turn his heart away from earthly treasure and fix his heart upon heavenly treasure—the undeserved grace and forgiveness of God. As a part of that inner change, together with true repentance, is the true and saving faith in Christ. "Come and follow me."

Jesus Himself called that young man to follow Him, but he "was sad at the saying, and went away grieved: for he had great possessions." Almost a disciple.

Alone with His disciples once more, Jesus said, "How difficultly shall those who have riches enter into the kingdom of God!" The disciples were amazed at His words. Jesus continued speaking, "Children, how difficult is it for those who trust in riches to enter the kingdom of God! It is easier for a camel to go through the eye of a needle, than for a rich man to enter into the kingdom of God." The disciples were dumbfounded. They looked at each other and said, "Who then can be saved?"

There was no doubt in the minds of the disciples but that Jesus meant exactly what He said. It *is* easier for a camel to go through the eye of a needle than for a rich man, one who trusts in riches, to enter into the kingdom of God. That was an absolute impossibility. Even though the disciples were poor in this world's goods they knew they were included because all men have a secret longing for the world's riches. They felt that Jesus was telling them, "Nobody can be saved." Jesus wants us to know that a rich man can do nothing for his salvation, nor can a poor man whose desire for riches is not dependent upon his possession of riches.

When in amazement they questioned Him, "Who then can be saved?" His answer was, "With men impossible!" All hope of our saving ourselves, in whole or part, must die. But Jesus has a word for us. When our hope dies and we realize our sin and our separation from God, then the gospel becomes real to us. "When sinners see their lost condition, and feel their pressing load of sin, Then Jesus cometh on His mission to heal the sinsick heart within." "With men impossible, but not with God! All things are possible with God!"

The day of miracles is not past. God can work a miracle in your heart and mine. Are you almost a disciple? Does human pride, or trust in material possessions blind you to the need of your soul? All have sinned and come short of the glory of God, but God hath made Him to be sin for us, who knew no sin; that we might be made the righteousness of God in Him.

All things are possible with God. Christ is able to save them to the uttermost that come unto God by Him. Are you almost a disciple? Or can you, by the grace of God, sing with Edward Mote:

> My hope is built on nothing less
> Than Jesus' blood and righteousness;
> I dare not trust the sweetest frame,
> But wholly lean on Jesus' name.
> On Christ, the solid rock, I stand;
> All other ground is sinking sand.

AMEN

NINETEENTH SUNDAY AFTER TRINITY

And he entered into a ship, and passed over, and came into his own city. And, behold, they brought to him a man sick of the palsy, lying on a bed: and Jesus seeing their faith said unto the sick of the palsy; Son, be of good cheer; thy sins be forgiven thee. And, behold, certain of the scribes said within themselves, This man blasphemeth. And Jesus knowing their thoughts said, Wherefore think ye evil in your hearts? For whether is easier, to say, Thy sins be forgiven thee; or to say, Arise, and walk? But that ye may know that the Son of man hath power on earth to forgive sins (then saith he to the sick of the palsy,) Arise, take up thy bed, and go unto thine house. And he arose, and departed to his house. But when the multitudes saw it, they marvelled, and glorified God, which had given such power unto men.

MATTHEW 9:1-8

Chapter Four

Be of Good Cheer

WHAT is there to cheer about?" is the cynical question of tormented people. Dark days of tragedy, trouble and war have been succeeded by black days of worry, hopelessness and despair. Housing trouble, the high cost of living, broken promises, family disaster, and ill health are the subjects of our latest grousings. "Why does God let everything happen to me?" is a constant refrain to most pastors. Internationally, the scene is little more encouraging with nihilism stalking much of Europe and Asia, and everywhere the constant threat of Marxian Communism with its inevitable bath of blood. Aldous Huxley's *Brave New World* has turned out to be a *Frightened, Fatigued Old World* and the crowning temptation is to be bitter and melancholy as our tale of woe grows. Little wonder that personal tensions keep mounting. A new Chicago mental hospital in its first month of operation had a thousand more applicants than it could handle. It is the inevitable result of the breakdown of an adequate reason for living.

"Be of good cheer" comes to our generation like the deep tones of an armistice. It is a more glorious announcement today than it was to the group which was gathered about Jesus as the palsied man was lowered through the roof into the presence of the Great Physician.

In the midst of ministering one morning to one of our hospitalized members, I was interrupted by the approach of one of Milwaukee's eminent surgeons. "I beg your pardon, Pastor," he said as he backed out. Realizing his eminence and his tremendous schedule, I suggested that I call on another while he checked the patient. He wouldn't hear of it. "Your presence here is far more important than mine," said he, as he closed the door again. A few moments later, we met in the hall. I told him how much I appreciated his attitude and how much his apparent faith in God had meant to the patient. "A cheerful heart is good medicine," I commented. "There is none better," he replied. "I have done all I can. Her recovery depends solely upon God and His gift of cheerfulness at the thought of living and fighting."

A cheerful heart is the best of medicines. It is sheer blasphemy, however, to suppose that cheerfulness can be acquired by will power or suggestion. To hang a motto "Keep Smiling" is an insult to a troubled soul. Superficial cheerfulness is a bubble that bursts when tragedy strikes. It is the empty husk before the spectre of the judgment seat of God.

Jesus Is the Christ, the Son of God

This parable of Jesus gives the basis of the only kind of cheer worth talking about. It is the third in a series of miracles. Each accumulates more evidence of the divinity of Christ until all heaven seems to explode in the acclaim that Jesus Christ is the Son of God, the Christ, the Savior of men, as He says, "Son, be of good cheer, thy sins are forgiven thee."

Any discerning student of the Bible is overwhelmed by the great number of claims Jesus made concerning His relationship with God the Father. "I and my Father are one." "I am sent from my Father." "He that hath seen me hath seen the Father," are but a few of the striking utterances of Jesus, the Son of God. The power placed in His hands according to His own admission either proves Him to be an egotistical impostor, or the Christ, the Son of God, as all Scripture acclaims Him.

In these rapidly moving miracles in St. Matthew He exercises convincing command over the physical laws of the universe. This undeniable, unique power matched with His miraculous birth attended by angels, the authority with which He spoke the truth of God ("Never before spake man like this"), His death, His resurrection, His transfiguration, and His ascension all bring one to the humble confession, "Truly, this is the Son of God."

Jesus was not attempting to conceal through subterfuge this truth concerning Himself as the all powerful Savior. Nor did He with false modesty try to dodge the Pharisees and the scribes. Consider His simplicity and directness when He said that it made no difference whether He obviously exercised control over the forces of nature, and said, "Take up thy bed and walk," or whether He manifested His Saviorhood by saying, "Son, thy sins be forgiven thee." As the Son of God He was in complete control of all.

No generation dares take the divinity of Jesus Christ for granted. The power of doubt and evil today is as malicious in deceitfulness as in the days when Jesus lived physically . . . as in the hearts of the witnesses of this miracle who in spite of observable evidence would not believe.

Just yesterday the mailman brought me some pamphlets from a man who claims to know the secret of God and man. Appealing to what he believes is a common-sense argument he writes, "We do not believe Almighty God made a mistake when he made this universe . . . to rectify that mistake drowned out the entire human race like rats in a trap. Neither do we believe that Almighty God created man in sin, and prescribed the only remedy to lie in believing the Almighty God was murdered on the cross to provide the only avenues of escape from an eternal doom in hell. . . . That is what 'Orthodoxy' teaches. It has a right to teach it if it wants to. We do not believe it and we do not teach it. What we do teach is this. . . . We teach that Almighty God, the Spirit that created this universe and man, actually lives in every created man and woman. The creeds of 'orthodoxy' naturally are very dear to it. But any man in his right mind knows that a new and more potent picture of God is necessary if this world is to be saved . . . we do not believe 'orthodoxy' has any ability actually to demonstrate the actual power of God in human lives. It is not necessary to believe anything orthodoxy teaches in order to *find* God . . . not one word is necessary to believe."

Such scripturally and theologically ignorant blasphemers deny that Jesus is God, that He is Savior. To lose Christ as the Son of God is to lose both God and heaven. Jesus, who had command over the laws of nature, who confessed with His own lips that He was the fulfiller of God's prophetic utterances, who revealed His sinlessness in His own stirring and convincing life, gave His life as a ransom for all. This Jesus, recognized universally as the greatest man that ever lived, is made nothing but a stupid fool, unless He is acclaimed the Son of God. Matthew, out of many eye-witness accounts chose this miracle to portray most clearly to men of every generation that Jesus is the Christ, the Son of God. As God, He alone has the power to forgive sin.

Man's Greatest Need Is Forgiveness

Browning said, "God's in His Heaven, all's right with the world." All was not right with the world. God had to come down from heaven to earth to do something about it. God visited His people and brought salvation. "Emmanuel—God with us," was the triumphant cry of the believers of old. "For God so loved the world that he gave his only begotten Son, that whosoever believeth in him should not perish, but have everlasting life." Thus Jesus had one supreme purpose, to reveal God's love and mercy toward fallen man.

God saw above all things that man's soul was disturbed and troubled by a guilty conscience. God saw man in relationship to Himself, and knew that man was in a helpless and hopeless state. "A lost and condemned creature" is Luther's description of what God viewed in man. It would never be possible for man to meet the problem of squaring his accounts with his Creator. Earth could not hold enough gold and precious things to pay the debt of man's sins and iniquities. Hence, God in His infinite love came down to help man, and to save him from his sins. For sin is man's fundamental problem.

In the highest circles of intellectualism man is recognized as fallen. The thinking man's creed asserts that man is his own worst enemy. Opinions as to how he fell and how he might rise again may be vastly divergent to the Christian faith. The fact remains that the world has never before been so jarred by the vicious consciousness of evil. The human individual is inadequate to combat the spirit of the age and control his demonic motives and passions. Man's need of a Savior is universally obvious.

In leaving the church one evening late last December, I heard the crash of steel against steel. Across the street a car had side-swiped a parked vehicle. Swerving back to the middle, bouncing up over the boulevard, crashing into a small tree with a tremendous clatter, the car turned over—the wheels spinning madly in the air. The driver apparently had given no thought to Jesus as Savior, nor himself as sinner. The police report showed he had taken his so-called Christmas cheer in liquid form. His car was out of control because he was out of control, and out of the control of God.

The wheels of commerce and industry will spin aimlessly until under the control of God. It is sin that draws us from God's control. Sin has separated and alienated man from God. That is why sin is man's fundamental problem. After all, if there is no sin, there can be no sinners. No sinners; no ruptured social relationships among men. Where there is no sin, there can be no selfishness, there can be no greed, there can be no cruelty in the heart of one toward another. Where there is no sin, there can be no sickness, no death; there can be no weeping, there can be no regrets. Where there is sin, there all the multitudinous evils follow it. Who can say that sin with its destructive sequence of havoc is not man's basic problem?

It was for the specific purpose of freeing man from the captivity of sin that God sent His only begotten Son Jesus Christ into the world. Jesus Christ came to reveal God's salvation. He was God's answer to man's need. Here in this glorious miracle He exercises His heaven-given love as He says, "Son, thy sins be forgiven thee." Little wonder all heaven broke loose when the good news burst into history, "For behold I bring you good tidings . . . for unto you is born this day in the city of David a Savior. . . ." It is through the forgiveness of sins that a warming, life-giving companionship is again possible between the righteous, holy God and sinful, frail, unholy man. Thus the words, "Son, thy sins be forgiven thee," are the greatest words human ears can hear. Are you in a position to hear these words from the lips of our Savior? If you are at the feet of Jesus

in repentance, you are hearing those life-given
words, and your paradise lost is now regained.

Cheerfulness Is the Inevitable
Result of Forgiveness

The Word of God that reveals Jesus Christ as
Savior has power to forgive and sustain. What
tragic losses and leaks occur in our spiritual lives
when we fail to live regularly and deeply into
God's saving Word.

An unused Bible was placed on the end table
of an all-too-typical home. A little son in the
family asked one day, "Whose book is this?"
"Why, God's book," replied the mother. "We
never use it, so shouldn't we give it back to Him?"
was her son's reply. This Book is no doubt in our
homes. Yet we so often act as though we could
bottle the grace of it in Baptism, or Confirmation or an Easter Communion. The power of
God's Word cannot remain fresh while stored in
the experience-tight closet of past commitments.
Forgiveness is a continuing attitude. Sin is effectively present. We sin much every day. Repentance, therefore, must be a frame of mind. Only
the dynamite of the law and the gospel in the
Word can humble us, forgive, and sustain us.
God's Word has power to sustain. The same Word
that relates, "Son, thy sins be forgiven thee," is
also the Word that says, "My grace is sufficient for
thee." "Rejoice in the Lord . . . make requests

known unto God . . ." cheers Paul. "I have strength for anything through Christ," he joyously chants. "This is the victory . . ." writes John concerning faith in Jesus Christ the living Word.

One of our consecrated lay visitors, a saint of God, waits day by day for the Lord to take her home. A heart ailment has kept her on the edge of death for over a year. Though tears sometimes flood her eyes, she smiles through her tears, for the victory over sin, death, and the devil is hers in Christ. Living daily in the Word, she lives in the joy of forgiveness, and the triumph of sustaining grace.

The doctor's verdict that you possess a fatal disease, the tragic news of death or disaster or failure never crushes one who lives in the forgiving, sustaining Word of God. It is the Word living in us that makes it true that, "Earth has no sorrow that heaven cannot heal."

Cheerfulness is the inevitable result of the forgiveness of sins. Cheerfulness is God's alternative to despair. It is the buoyant overflow of surging love and trust in the grace of God. It is inconceivable that one rightly related to God can possess an ugly disposition. With Jesus Christ in our heart . . . having drowned the Old Adam . . . there must be a quality if not a great degree of cheerfulness. Happiness is not cheerfulness. Cheerfulness runs deeper. Jesus was a man of sorrows and acquainted with grief. There is no happiness in many scenes, but He was always blessed with cheerfulness, because He knew He would conquer. In Christ we will win over sin and death. Rescued from sin and eternal death by Calvary's cleansing blood, how can we walk in uncheerfulness? We *must* walk in His steps. Kindness, unselfishness, love, patience, forgiving attitudes and the fruits of the Spirit are our necessity to bear. A glowing personality must be ours if we are living fully into the forgiveness of sins. It always brings cheer. It is the promise of Christ.

"Be of good cheer, thy sins be forgiven thee." It sounds most irrelevant to the sinner's mind. "This pitiful, palsied man needs health," is the lament of the unregenerate. But there is one thing more needful than physical health—the forgiveness of Christ. For more tragic by far than an invalided body is a dying soul.

A girl vacationing from Hollywood happened to be in Milwaukee during the International Luther League Convention. Knowing she was a skilled writer, I invited her to help with the convention. While she accepted graciously, I could easily see how such "all-out religion" as expressed in the theme *You Need Jesus Christ* nauseated her "finer tastes." Some months afterwards she frantically phoned my secretary for an immediate appointment with me. Her entrance was no longer measured and poised. A severe moral shock in her immediate circle of friends, for which she felt partially responsible, was shaking her like a leaf. As she dropped into a chair in my office she blurted out, "Pastor, I need Jesus Christ, oh, how I need Him! I must confess that during the Luther League convention I thought those thousands of young people naive and boorish. I felt sorry that they couldn't have been around a little more so that they would know better how much of religion to take so seriously. But now what I wouldn't give to change places with any one of them. If only I could sit under that theme now—because I do need Jesus Christ!"

Restless and dissatisfied through college, she had tried one thing after another. In Hollywood she thought she had found true satisfaction and cheerfulness. She was an above-average woman morally. Church attendance was always on her list of "musts." The life she lived is typical. Moving in the cocktail crowd, she became more and more indifferent to the sinfulness of sin and the need of Christ as the supplier of life and cheerfulness. Now a change had taken place. The shock she had received was doubled-barreled, for it also revealed her distance from Christ. It was more than drifting. Sin was a gnawing rat eating through the cords that bound her to Christ. She didn't return to Hollywood. She did return to Christ. One of the greatest satisfactions of my ministry is seeing regularly her face beaming the cheerfulness of a surrendered life in Christ. She is "exhibit A" in the numberless pages of Christ's book of miracles so vividly portraying that only the forgiveness of sin by the Divine Savior brings deep and lasting cheer.

It is not accidental that you fall at Jesus' feet to cry for forgiveness and sustaining power. His Holy Spirit calls you by the Gospel. Are you listening? Obeying? Then "be of good cheer, thy sins be forgiven thee."

AMEN

NINETEENTH SUNDAY AFTER TRINITY

And as Jesus passed by, he saw a man which was blind from his birth. And his disciples asked him, saying, Master, who did sin, this man, or his parents, that he was born blind? Jesus answered, Neither hath this man sinned, nor his parents: but that the works of God should be made manifest in him. I must work the works of him that sent me, while it is day: the night cometh, when no man can work. As long as I am in the world, I am the light of the world. When he had thus spoken, he spat on the ground, and made clay of the spittle, and he anointed the eyes of the blind man with the clay, And said unto him, Go, wash in the pool of Siloam, (which is by interpretation, Sent). He went his way therefore, and washed, and came seeing.

The neighbours therefore, and they which before had seen him that he was blind, said, Is not this he that sat and begged? Some said, This is he: others said, He is like him: but he said, I am he. Therefore said they unto him, How were thine eyes opened? He answered and said, A man that is called Jesus made clay, and anointed mine eyes, and said unto me, Go to the pool of Siloam, and wash: and I went and washed, and I received sight.

JOHN 9:1-11

Chapter Five

A Work of God

"ISN'T this the man who sat and begged?"
"Yes, it is."
"No, but he looks like him."
"I am he."
"How did it happen?"
"A man named Jesus said, 'Go and wash . . .'
I went and washed and received my sight."

This is your answer to the astonished, curious neighbors. You recall every happy, agonizing moment of it. He said, "Go . . ." You did go. You'll never be the same again since your meeting with this man Jesus. You are a new person, not only to the neighbors, but to yourself. Here you are in a new world with a new self—a self you couldn't see and didn't know, until your eyes were opened. Yes, you recall every moment of it.

It was an ordinary day. You really don't expect much to happen on an ordinary day.

You find your way to the same place in the

45

street. You know it by feel, a familiar feel aug-
mented by familiar sounds. You don't see anything, you just feel and hear, and smell—because
you are blind.

This goes on day after day, week after week.
Once in a while there's a new sound, a new smell,
and that's about all.

When there's a new sound, a new voice, it in-
trigues you. You try to figure out something about
the person or thing it belongs to; what kind of
a world *it* lives in. Sometimes there's a babble of
voices, the scent of a crowd, angry argument and
raucous laughter. You've been there long enough
to know whether it's a funeral procession, a wedding party, a group of rabbis, or a group of busi-
nessmen. Your insights have been sharpened. If
someone would ever ask you what you think—but
no one ever will, of course.

Then there's your own life. Your future. No
use of dwelling on that. There's nothing you can
do about it. Just build your world against the
other fellows, behind that wall of darkness. The
quiet anger that grips you is just something to
protect you against those sieges of self-pity and
loneliness, that sense of uselessness, the awful
frustration and futility.

If you could only see yourself as you really are.
You wonder what you would look like to yourself.
You'll never know. You've speculated about it.
It's hard to even guess. You've suspected that life

would be different. There's a self you've never really known. But —.

There's a babble again. It takes your mind off the self you do know. It's coming closer. Not a wedding procession. Not a group of argumentative rabbis. Closer now. There's quiet discussion. The owners are near now.

There's one voice that holds your attention.

They are very close. They have stopped. You just know they are looking at you in your wretchedness. What is it this time? More pity? More jokes? You are angry. This has happened a few times before. You wait for the sharp comments to come—those senseless, stupid speculations. They have been hard to bear lately, because of the haunting questions they raise in your own mind. There is nothing you can do. So you wait and listen, straining to sense what the sudden quiet might mean.

Then it comes. "Who sinned, this man or his parents?"

"Who sinned . . . who sinned . . .!" What business is it of theirs? You want to answer this yourself. You want the right answer. You want to silence these unseen intruders. Your soul cries out against them, but before you can shape the answer there is that voice you singled out. . . .

"Neither this man nor his parents." You hang upon those words. What more would He say? You want His full answer.

"Neither this man nor his parents: but that the works of God should be made manifest in him." What a strange answer to this age-old question. But they are speaking of you. Not someone else. What did He mean? Yes, of course, some people become sick and infirm because of their own sins. Some become sick and infirm because of the sins of others. Neither you nor your parents were to blame for this blindness. A deep sense of relief comes to you. But what about the latter part, "the works of God"?

Before you can think further, He is saying, "We must work the works of him that sent me, while it is day: the night comes when no man can work. When I am in the world, I am the light of the world."

Light of the world! Light . . .!

Something cool covers your eyes, but warm words fall upon your ears—words spoken just to you. "Go, wash in the pool of Siloam." You are saying to yourself, "I can't do it. I won't do it. It's just another disappointment. I'll tear this stuff from my eyes. I'll stop my ears. I'll curse the day I was born. It's hard enough to bear these inner tensions, to fight with myself day in and day out without this sort of disappointment. I'm lost and this man knows it. I'm sick of myself—the only self I've ever known. I must know for sure that He is speaking the truth before I'll do this!"

You're fighting something. Is it His promise?

His command? But His command has a promise
in it. His is another kind of voice. It seems to be
saying, Son, do this and you will know. Do and
you'll know! There's a note of urgency in His
voice, a note of authority in it. He is pleading
with you. He would be this way with anyone in
need, anyone sitting in darkness. It could be like
this if a man were spiritually blind.

This is no longer an ordinary day.

You start out before you weaken. If you *do* this
thing He has commanded, you'll *know* His promise. You know Siloam. You've been there before,
hoping against hope.

This is different. You feel the urgency of it, too.
You grope along with your heart beating faster
and faster. The fear of disappointment now becomes another kind of fear. This is a strange thing.
One fear for another. The fear of disappointment
for the fear of seeing yourself as you really are.
This self you've never known! Coming out of
darkness and into light, what would it be like?
What would *you* be like?

You are pushed, shoved along. You know the
pool is nearer. But you are back to where you
started from again. Cold, cruel doubt lays its
clammy tendrils around your mind, and you are
saying to yourself, "I can't go through with it. It
won't work. It can't work. Can't it? He said
'Go' and here I am. Have I done anything different from what I've done every morning? I've

started out on the promise of a new day. I haven't lived by my doubts, even in darkness. I've been living by the faith which is in me. However small it has been, I've still lived by that faith. Maybe He knows this, too. Yes, He must know it. I will have faith in His promise."

You crawl down to the water. His words are ringing in your ears.

"I am the light of the world. . . ."

Light!

You wash away the hard caked film and as it comes off, a weight is lifted. Now to open your eyes. Just a slit. Now a little more. First a haze. Then brilliance—so much that it's painful. Then there's movement. Everything is in a whirl. It's more than you can stand. But you fight through it. You want to see yourself as you really are, the self you haven't known all these years.

Slowly you look at the world around you with all its form and movement. It was yourself you wanted so desperately to see and know. Now you see that self with its rags and poverty, its uncleanness born of your own helplessness. Is this what others had seen all along? You know this is what He saw. But you are sure He had seen something else—something worth saving, the person you could be and were destined to be when your eyes were opened to see yourself as you really are. This is just the beginning. He has opened a whole new world. You are a new person. Not helpless any more. You have a grip on that new world because you have been given a new life.

With a song in your heart you go back to the old neighborhood.

The folks in the neighborhood did recognize you. You could tell them so much. Simple things with great consequences for them, too; things like doing in order to know; that His command always carries a promise; that obedience is akin to faith; that doubt always exists in the midst of our faith; that a person doesn't live by his doubts but by the faith which is in him. Yes, and more than this, rags, poverty, and uncleanness are outward symbols of something deep inside—something a person can't really see until his eyes are opened.

"A man that is called Jesus . . . said unto me, 'Go.'"

"I went . . . and received my sight."

A work of God!

AMEN

NINETEENTH SUNDAY AFTER TRINITY

And he was teaching in one of the synagogues on the sabbath.

And, behold, there was a woman which had a spirit of infirmity eighteen years, and was bowed together, and could in no wise lift up herself. And when Jesus saw her, he called her to him, and said unto her, Woman, thou art loosed from thine infirmity. And he laid his hands on her: and immediately she was made straight, and glorified God. And the ruler of the synagogue answered with indignation, because that Jesus had healed on the sabbath day, and said unto the people, There are six days in which men ought to work: in them therefore come and be healed, and not on the sabbath day. The Lord then answered him, and said, Thou hypocrite, doth not each one of you on the sabbath loose his ox or his ass from the stall, and lead him away to watering? And ought not this woman, being a daughter of Abraham, whom Satan hath bound, lo, these eighteen years, be loosed from this bond on the sabbath day? And when he had said these things, all his adversaries were ashamed: and all the people rejoiced for all the glorious things that were done by him.

LUKE 13:10-17

Chapter Six

She Went to Church

THERE is nothing unusual about going to church. We have grown up in it, and become accustomed to thinking of it as a fine tradition we have received from our forefathers, It is a national thing, and we cherish the thought "freedom to worship God," with the emphasis upon freedom. To see family after family arrive at church on Sunday morning, and one by one file into the pews, is the central attraction for many in going to church

We need to be reminded that the highest and noblest act of man is to worship God in truth and spirit. He created man, made him for this very purpose, and no man can alter this plan without hurting or harming his destiny. "Remember the Sabbath day, to keep it holy" is God's specific command to man. As a social, intellectual, and spiritual being, this instruction has a distinct and definite bearing upon his success in life.

When a factory sends out a new piece of machinery, it also sends instructions as to how it should be operated and looked after in order that the purchaser get the most benefit from it. God, who created man, has sent along His instructions for man's own good. God's laws are not something imposed upon man; they are principles and laws governing the relationship of the body to the mind, and mind to the soul of man. God's laws are for man's welfare. They are not something outside of man, but parts of his very life. To disregard them is to bring destruction upon his own life.

Our text speaks about a woman who went to church. There is nothing unusual about that—but let us take time to look at her. We may learn something profitable for our soul's welfare. It may remind us of the importance of going to church. The woman is described as one who had a spirit of infirmity for eighteen years. She was bowed together and could not lift herself up. It is a doctor who tells us this, Luke the physician. Surely, we must say, she was in need of charity; she was more fitted for a hospital than to be placed in the category of church-goer. Perhaps, just for this reason Luke gives this graphic description of her.

All experts on excuses for going to church should thoughtfully consider this woman. Can you see her struggling along? She had been sick for eighteen years. Her appearance, her manner of walk, her persistency of spirit to endure the ordeal, all reveal her emphasis upon the importance of the act. With all our modern conveniences and comfort, we need to ponder upon this woman's church-going before we offer our excuses.

She went to church. It was of great importance to her soul's welfare. Faith and obedience were active in her heart. Faith in God is important to our existence; it makes the difference between success and failure, between life and death. The test of faith is obedience.

There is little of such faith, hence obedience becomes difficult. We are a generation that knows, but we lack the power to live according to our knowledge. No other generation has heard so much preaching of God's Word. We hear, and yet we do not hear; we see, and yet we do not see; we know, and yet we do not know. The choice before us is obedience to God or death. Obedience is to hear the Word and live by the Word. We have become too wise in our own comfortable modern living. Our own understanding and reasoning has superseded obedience to God. Unbelief has tapped obedience out of our lives. Satan has out-witted our generation; he has woven his web around our will and understanding. Comfort and pleasure have become all-important. The Philistines are again at the Walls of Zion, and Delilah is playing her enticing game with Samson. Like Demas, the love of the present world has taken away the love for going to church. We think we are free. The fact of the matter is that Satan has bound us up in things of this world. We are too busy serving mammon. What is the remedy? Hear God's Word today. "Faith cometh by hearing, and hearing by the word of God." If there is to be obedience to God, we must again take time to hear His Word.

She went to church. She was in need and she was helpless. The spirit of infirmity had bowed her down, she was without strength of her own to rise. She was bound, but she longed for freedom. She was a daughter of Moses looking for the Consolation of Israel. Her church-going had brought her knowledge and understanding in the history of her people and in God's providence. No doubt, she had heard many of the promises concerning the coming of Messiah. Perhaps there was in her soul a dim light that gave her hope to look for the One who should heal the broken-hearted and set at liberty them that are bruised.

She went to church. Others have gone to church since. There is nothing unusual about that. The unusual entered when Jesus sought her out and the Liberator began to speak, when the power of the gospel of Jesus Christ began to work. Listen to the words of Jesus, "Woman, thou art loosed from thine infirmity." What a day! What a meeting! She had gone to church to find some words of comfort; instead, she met Him who had all power

When people take their church-going seriously, when men are loosed on the Sabbath, there will also be scoffers. If nothing happens, they scoff; if the unusual does happen, they scoff. They have been with the Church and will continue so in the future. We are thankful for their contribution; they have been helpful in the past and will be in the future. The ruler of the synagogue caused Jesus to give us helpful information regarding the Sabbath and its rightful place in the Christian's life. Criticism and opposition have always been helpful to Christians in awaking them from lethargy and spurring them on in search for truth.

In Mark 2:4 Jesus says, "The Sabbath was made for man and not man for the Sabbath. Therefore the Son of Man is the Lord of the Sabbath." As a steward over what God has created, man needs the Sabbath. It is essential for his stewardship. Just as air is essential for man's body to breath, so the Sabbath is essential for man's soul to live and perform his duties toward God. Earthly things have their place, but the Sabbath is for the spirit of man. Jesus is the Lord of the Sabbath. It was made for man, but never given to man. It is to be used by man, but it is the Lord's day to be devoted to His service and honor. The woman of our text went to church on the Sabbath. She had been there before. She had sung many of the Psalms before, but on this day all took a new aspect. New life had come and there was a new song in her mouth. "Bless the Lord, O my soul, and forget not all his benefits" was no longer just a national thing. It was something that fitted her soul. She honored and glorified her God in presenting her own soul to God in a sacrifice of thanksgiving. She used the day to honor her God.

She went to church. Her going there brought life and salvation. We do not know any more about her. Luke's description of her ends by saying she glorified God. That's all we know, but it is the most important thing. Holy Writ has many such unnamed worshippers. They are defined for us as "a man," "a woman," "a leper," etc. Their personal names do not occur. The important thing about them was that they came, they met Jesus, and they received help. Like the woman of our text, there have been many church-goers since, who though they were bound, have been set free through the gospel. We do not know their names. That is not important. The important thing is that their church-going brought them to Jesus and He set them free. Once Jesus told a parable about two men that went to church. The one went there to tell God how good he was; the other went to be set free from his sins. Jesus said about the latter, he went home from church justified, set free.

The woman went to church. There is nothing unusual about that. The unusual thing was that she was set free. AMEN

TWENTIETH SUNDAY AFTER TRINITY

And Jesus answered and spake unto them again by parables, and said, The kingdom of heaven is like unto a certain king, which made a marriage for his son, And sent forth his servants to call them that were bidden to the wedding: and they would not come. Again, he sent forth other servants, saying, Tell them which are bidden, Behold, I have prepared my dinner: my oxen and my fatlings are killed, and all things are ready: come unto the marriage. But they made light of it, and went their ways, one to his farm, another to his merchandise: And the remnant took his servants, and entreated them spitefully, and slew them. But when the king heard thereof, he was wroth: and he sent forth his armies, and destroyed those murderers, and burned up their city. Then saith he to his servants, The wedding is ready, but they which were bidden were not worthy. Go ye therefore into the highways, and as many as ye shall find, bid to the marriage. So those servants went out into the highways, and gathered together all as many as they found, both bad and good: and the wedding was furnished with guests.

And when the king came in to see the guests, he saw there a man which had not on a wedding garment: And he saith unto him, Friend, how camest thou in hither not having a wedding garment? And he was speechless. Then said the king to the servants, Bind him hand and foot, and take him away, and cast him into outer darkness; there shall be weeping and gnashing of teeth. For many are called, but few are chosen.

MATTHEW 22:1-14

Chapter Seven

For Many Are Called, But Few Chosen

"FOR many are called, but few chosen." What a startling word—a startling summing up of one of our Lord's kingdom parables.

"God would have all men to be saved and to come unto the knowledge of the truth." Therefore He sent His only begotten Son into the world, "that whosoever believeth in him should not perish, but have everlasting life." There is not a human being of any age, race, nationality or class for whom the gospel is not intended. The Christ of the gospel is a Savior who stands with open arms inviting all to come to Him, "Come unto me, all ye that labor and are heavy laden, and I will give you rest!"

Yet, of all who are called, only few are chosen! How can it be?

One thing is certain; there is no such thing as an arbitrary predestination, or election, to damnation. To teach anything of that kind is to fly in the face of all that God through Jesus Christ has let us know about Himself and His kingdom. Since God would have all men to be saved, and sends forth His messengers to proclaim a universal gospel, men alone are to blame if they fail to obtain eternal life. We must add that nothing shows more clearly how the human heart has been bedeviled by sin than the refusal of many to accept the salvation God has made possible through Christ, and which He offers as a free gift to all, bad and good alike.

Let us look at our gospel, this parable of the Marriage of the King's Son. We shall find the answer to the question, Why, when God would have all men to be saved, are so few chosen, and so many rejected?

The King in the parable, we understand, is God. The wedding feast is that abundance of grace, forgiveness, freedom, cleansing, joy, strength, courage, hope, which God has made available for every man, woman, and child, through His Son, our Lord and Savior, Jesus Christ. Christ's giving of Himself on Calvary's cross is the supreme manifestation of that overflowing love of God by which He desires to draw all of His fallen and lost children unto Himself. The gospel is an earnest invitation to our whole race, "Behold, all things are ready: Come to the marriage feast."

The parable presents the King as sending forth His servants "to call them that were bidden to the marriage feast." To these the invitation had been given in advance. Now the King's servants are sent to remind them of the invitation and to tell them "that all things were ready." They "make light" of the invitation. These, however, are not the only ones the King would have at His Son's marriage feast. So the servants are sent out "into the highways" to bid others, not previously invited, "as many as they should find," and to gather them. "And the wedding was furnished with guests."

This parable was spoken at the time when the enmity of the Jewish leaders to Jesus was nearing its climax. These Jews and their leaders, members of God's chosen people, had been nourished upon the Messianic promises of the Old Testament. Their Messiah was now in their midst. They should have recognized in Him the characteristics of Isaiah's Servant of the Lord. But they wanted a warrior king, not a humble, suffering Servant, and now they were about to reject Him. Jesus desires to open their eyes to the enormity of the crime they are about to commit, hoping that some of them might still be saved as brands from the burning. In any event, they are not going to be able to excuse themselves and say that they had not been warned.

Those who were gathered in from the highways and byways may be thought of as the publicans and harlots whom the self-righteous Pharisees despised, and the Gentiles whom the Jews in their smug nationalistic pride looked upon as dogs unfit for a place in the kingdom of God. We must not for a moment read the parable as if the salvation of these social outcasts, and of the Gentiles, were an afterthought with God, something He thought of since His "chosen people" made light of His grace. The book of Jonah in particular, but other portions of the Old Testament as well, emphatically brings out that when God chose Israel to be in a special way His people, He was not giving them a monopoly on the kingdom. They were to be custodians of God's revelation, a missionary people, responsible for sharing their spiritual heritage with the nations about them.

Applying the parable to ourselves, we who have been brought up in the Christian Church, we who have been baptized, instructed in the Word, and who have been under the constant influence of the gospel and enjoyed the privileges of fellowship with Christian people, we are those to whom the invitation has gone out, and who are reminded that "all things are ready" and urged to "come to the marriage feast." The tragic fact is that many of us make light of the invitation, and thus bring God's judgment down upon ourselves.

Strange and sad, is it not, that many of us make light of the kingdom?

It is not without deep significance that the kingdom of God is likened to a marriage banquet. A wedding stands for joy. Wedding guests rejoice with the bride and groom. They rejoice, too, with their host, and with their fellow guests. When the kingdom of God is likened to a wedding banquet, it is because the kingdom of God is joy. We often think of its Founder as "a man of sorrows, acquainted with grief." He was that. But do we stop to consider to how great an extent His life was a song of joy? We read of Him that He "rejoiced in the spirit." He found joy in the beauties of nature, in human relations like those of a happy family, in fellowship with His friends, and above all in the consciousness of oneness with His heavenly Father. Even in the midst of agonizing pain He knew a joy that made it possible for Him to endure the cross and despise the shame of His suffering (Heb. 12:2). Cleaving to God's will, the bitter vicarious suffering on the cross was turned into joy in the consciousness that He was fulfilling His Father's plan for the redemption of our fallen race.

It is to joy God invites us. That is the reason His invitation is called "gospel," or "good news." To be sure, acceptance of the invitation is accompanied with the pain of repentance and the fire of shame, as we confess our sin and guilt to God and men. But these fires are refining fires, and prepare us for the great joys that follow. Forgive ness and guilt removed become a fountain of joy welling up unto eternal life. God finds a dwelling place in the heart of the forgiven one, and His presence brings joy even in the hour of tribulation. Winds of adversity may stir up bil-lows on life's surface. In the depths of the heart, however, is peace and joy in the consciousness that, having said *Yes* to God's call, we are His. We are His in spite of our total unworthiness. He will make all things work out for our good. Exulting in that confidence which faith has in Him, the troubled soul makes the Psalmist's words his own, "Yea, though I walk through the valley of the shadow of death, I will fear no evil: for thou art with me; thy rod and thy staff they com-fort me."

This joy of the kingdom of God is spurned— spurned, alas, by multitudes who have heard the gospel through years of contact with the Christian Church.

You see, the joys of the kingdom of God are not the sensuous joys which carnal men seek. As the apostle Paul reminds us, "The kingdom of God is not meat and drink; but righteousness, and peace, and joy in the Holy Ghost."

"Meat and drink"—this expression stands for our bodily and temporal needs. Since God has given us bodies to dwell in while here on earth, we need food, clothing, shelter. The body is not to be neglected. God not only wants us to give decent care to our own bodies, but also to be solicitous for the bodily welfare of our more unfortunate brethren, whether at home or in foreign lands. But what a perversion of values it is if we allow solicitude for the needs and pleasures of these bodies, which soon must die, to blind us to the far greater importance of our immortal souls! "What is a man profited, if he shall gain the whole world, and lose his own soul? or what shall a man give in exchange for his soul?"

It is not only a question of the life hereafter. For the riches and pleasures of this world, if pursued for their own sake, give no lasting joy even here. They pall on the one who pursues them, until he sooner or later finds out, with the author of Ecclesiastes, that all these things are "vanity and vexation of spirit," and that they destroy the soul and leave one without any true joy in this life, to say nothing about something to cling to when we come to the end of our short time on earth. The only deep and lasting joy, the joy which "shall not be taken from us," is that which comes to him who knows himself to be God's forgiven and restored child, living in fellowship with Him and under His constant care, guidance and protection, in a life devoted to His service.

To be sure, many who lose themselves in the

pursuit of material things and sensuous pleasure are troubled in conscience. More or less vaguely they realize that they are not putting first things first. They gamble with the thought of first enjoying to the full the sensuous pleasures of the flesh. They intend to turn to Christ some day, soon enough to escape being cast out into the "outer darkness where there shall be weeping and gnashing of teeth." To what blindness and perversity such thoughts bear witness! In effect they say, "The fresh foliage and ripe fruit of youth and vigorous manhood we will give to the devil. God will no doubt be satisfied with the sere leaves and shrivelled fruit of our old age." What an affront to God! What self-deception! Such blind souls do not find the joy that satisfies even in this life, for that comes only to him who surrenders to God, confesses his sin, accepts Christ, and dedicates his life to His service. Furthermore, it is well to remember that, while God's grace will not be denied the deathbed penitent, the only record of a last moment conversion in all Scripture is that of the robber on the cross. No one has any guarantee that such an opportunity will be given him.

Let us be frank and face ourselves honestly. You know there is nobody we so easily fool as ourselves. Let us be done "kidding" ourselves.

When the servants came to "them that were

bidden to the wedding" and reminded them that "all things were ready," the invited guests "made light of it, and went their ways, one to his farm, another to his merchandise." Some even "took his servants, and treated them spitefully, and slew them."

This is all happening today, too, and among us.

Perhaps not many actually do physical violence to the messengers of the gospel, at least not in our supposedly "civilized" society. Figuratively, however, there are more than enough who slay the servants of the Lord by trying to shoot holes in their reputations, sneer at them, and belittle their work.

How about those who "go to their farms and to their merchandise" rather than heed the gospel invitation? Do you think they are few?

We speak about "owning" property. How often the supposed owner proves to be not the owner, but the owned! We glut and feast our eyes and hearts on farms, houses, bank deposits, stocks, bonds, and say, "All of this is *mine, mine!*" We think of our businesses as gold mines from which we are going to take more and more of the stuff we like to pile up in the delusion that it is going to make us happy. In the process we become more and more selfish, and less and less concerned for the welfare of our neighbor and the glory of God. Perhaps we try to delude ourselves with the thought that we are practical men, and say to ourselves that "nothing succeeds like success." If we were not so blind, we should see that nothing fails so completely as what the world worships as success. By its distorted sense of values, and by making light of life's spiritual meaning, it kills the soul. When mammon, property, becomes our god and master, we are not free. We are no longer owners, but owned, and by our allegiance to this false god, exclude ourselves from the kingdom.

But the King's Son's wedding banquet shall be furnished with guests, even though you and I should be missing.

"They which were bidden were not worthy. Go ye therefore into the highways, and as many as ye shall find, bid to the marriage." The result? "The wedding was furnished with guests."

What kind of guests? Many of them could not boast of having belonged to the possessing classes. Some of them were ne'er-do-wells. Among them were many against whom some churches would draw the color line. Yes, and there were publicans and harlots, social outcasts and moral derelicts—criminals, too, deserving a life sentence in a penitentiary.

What? Does God prefer riff-raff and criminals to nice, respectable people? Not at all. Nevertheless, Jesus said to the nice, law-observing, tithing, church-going Pharisees, "Publicans and harlots go into the kingdom of God before you." That is not because He takes delight in their sins and vices, but because they are much more likely to be dissatisfied with the lives they are leading, and therefore more likely to be longing for something better. Disillusioned as to any hope of finding satisfaction in the possession of goods, or in the indulgence of the flesh, they are more receptive to a gospel which promises them cleansing, forgiveness, freedom, self-respect, strength, and eternal hope.

When churches become smug middle-class clubs, as sometimes happens, they forget that God would have the gospel brought to the poor, the social outcasts, the underprivileged, the less respectable, the morally derelict, and those of other colors, races, and nationalities.

What nice respectable churches have sometimes failed to do, groups like the Salvation Army have often done in their stead. They have helped to "furnish the wedding guests." You may be familiar with Vachel Lindsay's poem, "General Booth Enters Heaven." What an entourage he is described as bringing with him!

> Walking lepers followed, rank on rank
> Lurching bravoes from the ditches dank,
> Vermin-eaten saints with mouldy breath,
> Unwashed legions from the ways of death.

You and I would perhaps have considered ourselves too good to go near such social outcasts, much less bring them the gospel invitation to become citizens of the kingdom of God. Jesus never despised this class of people, nor did His servant, General Booth. He knew what they, by the transforming grace of God, could become.

General Booth, in Vachel Lindsay's poem, enters heaven with followers born anew, and by the power of the gospel made into new men and women fit for the kingdom.

> . . . in an instant all that blear review
> Marched on spotless, clad in raiment new.
> The lame were straightened, withered limbs uncurled
> And blind eyes opened on a new bright world.

Such is the miracle of the gospel accepted in faith, and how thankful we should be that the gospel is just that kind of power unto salvation. Since we have that kind of gospel, let no one say, "This man, or that, is too hopelessly fallen; there can be no room at the heavenly banquet for such as he." No, not even if he is familiar with the vilest of sins and besmirched with the filthiest of vices. When the gospel invitation comes to such a one, or to you and me, there is only one thing that can keep us out of the heavenly banquet hall. We can make light of the gospel, and thus shut ourselves out.

Turning again to our parable, we take note of one who came to the wedding banquet, but was thrown out.

The wedding banquet of the King's Son was prepared with lavish hospitality. The guests were assembled, resplendently robed for the feast and waiting for the royal host to enter. As the King enters His eye immediately falls upon one who was dressed in everyday attire, as if he had just come from his "farm" or his "merchandise," a man with no sense of fitness, and neglectful of decent proprieties. The King challenges him, but in a spirit of kindness. "Friend," he calls him, and says to him, "How camest thou in hither not having a wedding garment?" The man is speechless. He has no excuse for his rudeness. Others made light of the invitation and stayed away. This man made light of it and came. So the King says to His servants, "Bind him hand and foot, and take him away, and cast him into the outer darkness; there shall be weeping and gnashing of teeth."

Was not the King unduly harsh? Perhaps the man had no money with which to buy a wedding garment, and came in the best he had.

Among oriental kings it was customary to give wedding garments to their guests. Thus there was no excuse for the man who came attired in his own everyday clothes.

In the churches of today are there any, do you suppose, like this man who "had not a wedding garment"?

Are there not men of worldly spirit, unappreciative of the blessings and joys of the kingdom

of God, folks who think there may be some benefit to be derived from outward connection with
the people of God, and therefore "belong" to some
church? They may go through the motions of
religion, but their hearts are far away. They may
have the appearance of serving God, but secretly
their hearts belong to their "farm" or their "merchandise." They really do not feel at home among
the twiceborn.

Let no one say, therefore, that it is impossible
for a loving heavenly Father to cast anyone out
into the outer darkness of hell. God desires no
man's damnation. But men damn themselves by
making light of the kingdom of God. God would
have no slaves in His kingdom, and were He to
compel anyone to enter heaven, heaven itself
would be turned into hell for that soul. Thus God
has no choice but to consign those earth-bound
souls to the outer darkness they have chosen for
themselves.

The kingdom of God is joy unspeakable; it
is peace, assurance, strength, and a "hope that
maketh not ashamed." God calls all to share in
these blessings. Not only that, but the very gospel
through which He calls us is "the power of God"
through which His Holy Spirit also awakens, en-
lightens, sanctifies, and preserves all who respond
to it. God leaves nothing undone.

Therefore, when the sinner who realizes the

vanity and fleeting nature of things temporal and
material, and longs to be set free, responds to the
invitation, and says, in the words of Charlotte
Elliott,

> Just as I am, without one plea
> But that Thy blood was shed for me,
> And that Thou bidst me come to Thee,
> O Lamb of God, I come, I come.
>
> Just as I am, and waiting not
> To rid my soul of one dark blot,
> To Thee whose blood can cleanse each spot,
> O Lamb of God, I come, I come.

he shall hear words of blessed welcome, "Come,
ye blessed of my Father! Inherit the kingdom prepared for you from the foundation of the world."

AMEN

TWENTIETH SUNDAY AFTER TRINITY

Again, the kingdom of heaven is like unto treasure hid in a field; the which when a man hath found, he hideth, and for joy thereof goeth and selleth all that he hath, and buyeth that field.

Again, the kingdom of heaven is like unto a merchant man, seeking goodly pearls: Who, when he had found one pearl of great price, went and sold all that he had, and bought it.

Again, the kingdom of heaven is like unto a net, that was cast into the sea, and gathered of every kind: Which, when it was full, they drew to shore, and sat down, and gathered the good into vessels, but cast the bad away. So shall it be at the end of the world: the angels shall come forth, and sever the wicked from among the just, And shall cast them into the furnace of fire; there shall be wailing and gnashing of teeth.

MATTHEW 13:44-50

Chapter Eight

The Kingdom and You

IN THE chapter from which our text is taken, the Lord by means of seven parables emphasizes some important truths concerning the kingdom He came to establish. The fact that there are seven in one group seems to be intentional, this sacred number symbolizing God's rule of grace in the world of men.

Our text consists of the last three of these seven parables, each one dealing with the kingdom of heaven. Together they show not only how the individual acquires the kingdom, but also how the gospel seeks to draw all men unto God. By means of the parable of the tares among the wheat, the Lord has just pointed out the fearful fate in store for those who stand in a false relationship to the kingdom, as well as the blessedness of those who are its true children. Therefore make certain, He would seem to add, make certain that you yourself become a partaker of the kingdom. Take

no offense because here on earth both good and
bad are gathered together. On the last day they
shall become separated. Rejoice over this that
the kingdom-net, the gospel, seeks to gather *all*,
therefore also *you*.

The Kingdom-Treasure Is at Hand— Have You Found It?

In ancient days, especially in the East, the practice of hiding valuable treasures was common.
This was due to frequent wars and ravaging robber bands. Thus it could happen that with some
wealthy man's sudden death all trace of his buried
wealth was lost until by accident another stumbled
upon it. That is the situation in this parable.

That the hoard was hidden in a field brings out
the thought that God did not hide His treasure
far off in the heavens where no human being
could even come near it, but in a common, lowly
place, where discovery was possible. One man
found it. He was one of the "whosoever"s so often
named in the Scriptures. He was one in whose
place you may write your own name. The finding
itself excludes all human merit and seems accidental. But God placed the treasure and so guided
the man that he found it.

The field in which the *spiritual* treasure may
be found is the church in which the Word of God
is taught in its truth and purity, and the sacraments are rightly administered. Many walk about

in this field year after year without finding the true treasure. They hear of the glory of the kingdom, of the grace of Christ, and of heavenly treasures. Still, nothing of this seems real to them.

Perhaps you can remember the day when you did meet God in a special way; when a word concerning death and damnation passed like a sharp sword through your soul, and you began to yearn for something you could rely upon both in life and in death. Perhaps it was a word concerning the love of Christ which came to you with such compelling force that you never again could forget it. It took on living reality, and represented just what your heart was longing for, the forgiveness of sins in Christ Jesus with resulting peace and joy in the Holy Spirit. It matters not where or how such an experience comes to you. The thing to remember is that *when God and man meet, it is D-day for the soul*. Its eternal destiny hangs in the balance

Luther was seeking peace for his soul when he found the Bible, seemingly by accident. Forsaking everything else, he devoted himself to an intensive study of the newly found volume, and discovered in it a treasure that liberated his own soul and enabled him to uncover God's way of salvation by faith alone. The meaning of the cross was all but lost in a wilderness of traditions and commandments of men. For Luther to oppose the selling of indulgences, to defy the papal bull of excommunication, and to spite the wrath of the highest and most powerful authorities of the land meant that he risked his all in constant demonstration of having found a treasure which nothing and nobody could take away from him: ". . . And should they, in the strife, take kindred, goods and life, we freely let them go, they profit not the foe; with us remains the kingdom."

You, too, may find the treasure between the covers of your own holy Bible. As the field which the man purchased doubtless was similar to neighboring fields, yet contained underneath the surface a treasure which the others did not have, so the Bible, in outward appearance little different from other books, contains a treasure found nowhere else. According to the "disciple whom Jesus loved" it was written in order that you should believe that Jesus is the Christ, the Son of God, and that through this faith you might have eternal "life in his name."

The Kingdom-Pearl Is for Sale— Have You Bought It?

The second parable deals with a merchant who one day discovered a precious pearl. The price of it was so great that it called for everything he had. But he knew it was worth it, and gladly closed the bargain.

It is striking, indeed, that Jesus would compare the kingdom of heaven to a pearl, especially when we consider the nature and the characteristics of pearls. Genuine pearls are the result of suffering. They are found in clam and oyster shells which have been bruised accidentally or by an enemy. When a wound has been inflicted, the little animal seeks to heal that wound by the secretion of a certain fluid which gradually develops into that precious material from which such costly gems are made.

The kingdom of heaven was made an obtainable reality to you and me through the suffering of Christ. That suffering was no mere accident. No, it was planned before the beginning of creation, and was included in God's promise to Adam in the Garden of Eden. Isaiah, among many others, saw it clearly. He speaks of the one who was wounded for our transgressions and bruised for our iniquities.

> There is a fountain filled with blood
> Drawn from Immanuel's veins,
> And sinners plunged beneath that flood
> Lose all their guilty stains.
>
> WM. COWPER

Like the man who found the great treasure in the field, the merchant knew nothing of "the pearl of great price." But he *found* it. Where, when, and how makes no difference; it all seems accidental and yet is not. God had a hand in it. He lets even those who seek valuable things in the world "find" Christ.

In the expressions "goodly pearls" and "one pearl of great price" the thought is that Christ and His salvation are to be ranked with the very highest and best in this world. They are a pearl among pearls. Indeed, this pearl absolutely outranks all other pearls the world has ever seen. It is "one"; there is and can be no second. It is therefore really beyond all price, beyond any possible equivalent.

When the parable says that the merchant sold all his former pearls, it means that his whole heart was transferred from other noble interests to the one supreme interest, Christ. To sell all that one has in order to obtain the kingdom is necessary and understandable. If there exists something which I value so highly that I am not willing to part with it to obtain the kingdom of heaven, it proves that the kingdom is not of supreme importance to me. But then it is not mine either, for the Lord will not tolerate being assigned second place in my affection.

There is a difference between being rich in the Lord and rich in the world. Great worldly riches commonly multiply the owner's concern lest he through some financial transaction either on the part of himself or others should lose his wealth and be reduced to poverty. He who is rich in the Lord, however, possesses a peace of mind and heart which the world is utterly unable to understand.

Only he who has found the pearl of great price

is prepared for the future. When the angels shall come forth to separate the wicked from the right-eous, the question will not concern one's station in this world, but whether or not one has found and kept the "pearl of great price"—whether one is in deed and in truth a child of God.

The Kingdom-Net Is Being Filled— Are You in It?

"Again, the kingdom of heaven is like unto a net, that was cast into the sea, and gathered of every kind.'

The net spoken of here is not of the kind which is thrown out in a semicircle and then immediate-ly pulled ashore; nor is it one put out where the fish may be chased into it. Here we are dealing with a type of net which is let down into the sea (the Sea of Galilee, not the Mediterranean) and kept there for some time, until so many fish have become entangled in its meshes that it must be taken up. What follows is an ordinary scene in the activities of fishermen: the net hauled to the beach and the gathering of the "good" fish into vessels while the "bad" are "cast away."

This parable deals with all those who are caught in the gospel net. Men of all kinds and conditions are swept into its meshes. Here on earth they are mixed together in the outward body of the church. They all confess and profess faith, but not all are pronounced "righteous" by the divine Judge.

Some are hypocrites, sham Christians, mere adherents of the church.

In actual fishing, the fishermen handle the net and pick out the good fish. The gospel is proclaimed by the church, God's own institution, but God Himself has ordained that the separation of the godly from the wicked is to be made by angels chosen by Him for that purpose. The fishermen, the workers in God's kingdom on earth, are reminded that it is not their task to have charge of the final separation between the "good" and the "bad," between the saved and the lost. God alone knows each individual heart.

Peter once said, "Depart from me, for I am a sinful man, O Lord." In the language of our parable it amounted to saying, Cast me away, for I am a dead fish. The Lord did not cast him away, however, for in Peter's heart there was an unspoken cry for mercy and pardon. God resists the proud, but gives grace to the humble.

In addition to the instruction which it conveys, the parable is intended as a mighty warning. You who are in contact with the gospel, what kind of fish are you? How will the judgment day find you? What if you should be thrown into "the furnace of fire"? Every proclamation of "the kingdom of heaven" is a call to repent and to accept the righteousness by faith in Christ and thus become "righteous." The wickedness of "the wicked" lies in this very point; outwardly they accept the gospel, but inwardly refuse to repent and to rest their faith on Christ.

The net is being filled and will be taken up some day. Then the angels of heaven shall come forth, and "sever the wicked from among the righteous." It is a terrible fact that many who were in contact with the net either through some outward church organization, or in some other way, will then be found dead spiritually, and just as useless as dead and decayed fish. No more than a dead fish can avoid being cast away, no more can a soul dead "in trespasses and sins" avoid being thrown out into what Jesus here calls "the furnace of fire" where there shall be "the weeping and gnashing of teeth." The heavenly mansions are only for the living, not for the dead.

What is *your* relationship to the kingdom?

With threefold emphasis Christ in these parables shows you that the kingdom with all its treasures is being offered you "without money and without price." Is it yours today?

AMEN

TWENTIETH SUNDAY AFTER TRINITY

Hear another parable: There was a certain house-holder, which planted a vineyard, and hedged it round about, and digged a winepress in it, and built a tower, and let it out to husbandmen, and went into a far country: And when the time of the fruit drew near, he sent his servants to the husbandmen, that they might receive the fruits of it. And the husbandmen took his servants, and beat one, and killed another, and stoned another. Again, he sent other servants more than the first: and they did unto them likewise. But last of all he sent unto them his son, saying, They will reverence my son. But when the husbandmen saw the son, they said among themselves, This is the heir; come, let us kill him, and let us seize on his inheritance. And they caught him, and cast him out of the vineyard, and slew him. When the lord therefore of the vineyard cometh, what will he do unto those husbandmen? They say unto him, He will miserably destroy those wicked men, and will let out his vineyard unto other husbandmen, which shall render him the fruits in their seasons. Jesus saith unto them, Did ye never read in the scriptures, The stone which the builders rejected, the same is become the head of the corner: this is the Lord's doing, and it is marvellous in our eyes? Therefore say I unto you, The kingdom of God shall be taken from you, and given to a nation bringing forth the fruits thereof. And whoso-ever shall fall on this stone shall be broken: but on whomsoever it shall fall, it will grind him to powder.

MATTHEW 21:33-44

Chapter Nine

How Long Can God Bless America?

MANY of us are asking this question today. We are wondering, "Who will survive and lead? Will it be atheist Russia, or a Christian America?"

Our text was written to a nation that had refused to honor Christ and was about to go to ruin. "The kingdom of God shall be taken away from you," says Jesus to the Jewish leaders. "It will be given to a nation producing the fruits of it."

God has been good to America. Many of us are familiar with the song, "God Bless America." Hundreds of thousands of copies have been sold since it was written in the critical days before the last war. Sung thoughtlessly by many, prayerfully by some, it has become one of our popular national songs. Today let us ask ourselves the question, *How long can God bless America?*

87

One answer we find in the first parable in our text told by Jesus. The answer is *as long as we give God the fruits due Him.*

The vineyard in ancient Palestine was just as common and as important as the family farm in America today. Therefore, Jesus tells His enemies, the leaders of the Jews, a story about a vineyard. The householder in this story is God. The vineyard is His revealed religion. The hedge is the Ten Commandments, separating God's people from the surrounding pagan nations. The fruits are the results of true religion: repentance, faith, and Christian living. The tenants of the vineyard are the Jewish people and their leaders.

When the vineyard had been planted long enough so that God could expect a harvest, He sent His servants. Samuel, David, and others went and sought for the harvest in the name of their Lord. They found little fruit. Then He sent a long series of prophets. They were mistreated and put to death by the Jewish leaders. Tradition tells us that Isaiah was sawed in two. Jeremiah was exiled to Egypt and killed there. Last of all, God sent His Son. But even as Jesus speaks to them, the leaders of the people were plotting to put Him also to death. Jesus knows this and says so, looking them right in the eye as He speaks. There is tension and drama in this conversation.

Thus the spiritual leaders of the religion of Israel plotted to pervert it into a religious racket for themselves. They killed Christ, just as the wicked sharecroppers killed the heir, thinking they could thus protect themselves. As a result, the vineyard was removed from among them.

First, a terrible national calamity came upon them. In 70 A.D. the city of Jerusalem was taken and razed by the Roman general, Titus. Hundreds of thousands of its citizens were massacred. The temple, the center of the Old Testament religion, was battered to the ground.

Then the final spiritual calamity fell. They lost fulfillment of their religion. They rejected Christ. As a nation to this day, they have never found their Messiah.

But when the Lord punished Israel, He did not let the vineyard itself be laid waste. On the contrary, He took steps to make it more fruitful than before. This vineyard became the New Testament religion of Christ. This wonderful possession God gave to the Gentiles. In its most active and vital form it passed on to the European peoples, and to us in this God-blessed land of America.

What kind of stewards have we been of the blessings of our faith?

Surely we began and grew as a Christian nation. The United States was settled, not by Communists or freethinkers, but by Christians. The Supreme Court of the United States has officially stated, "This is a Christian nation." The founding fathers, the original charters, the early practices throughout the country were distinctively Christian. Many of us visited the Freedom train when it passed through our communities recently. We saw there the priceless documents of our democratic heritage. Not many of the hundreds of thousands who visited the train realize that the Declaration of Independence itself closes with a declaration of our *dependence* upon God. We have been richly blessed through the Bible, through the Savior, through the gospel. This harvest season of the year reminds us of our blessings. We are the land of freedom and opportunity. We have never started a war, yet we have never lost a war in which we became involved. We emerged from this last war in a position of tremendous leadership and influence, not just because we had the bomb, but because we were a nation whose God is the Lord.

But how long can God continue to bless America? Can He bless us while our divorce rate is at the ratio of one to every three marriages? True, some of our religious statistics are encouraging. About thirty-five per cent of the American people were reported as church members in 1895. Over fifty per cent of them are church members now. On the other hand, think of the tide of Bible-hating, Christ-denying Modernism which has swept away whole denominations. Modernism is so strong in present day Protestantism that we felt it necessary to stay out of the World Council of

Churches for confessional reasons. This in spite of the many practical advantages we could have gained. Isn't it true that America stands more and more sure of herself and less and less interested in Jesus Christ?

How long can God bless our congregations? Our Church has grown wonderfully in the past few years. How vital is the Christian fruit of many of our congregations, however, when they have never given one minister or a missionary to God's work?

How long can God bless our homes, the foundation of our nation? "God bless our home" is a motto I have seen in many of your homes. A beautiful prayer and reminder it is to all who go in and out. But how large a place does God have on your reading table, in your checkbook? How much does He have to say in your plans for educating your children? How often do you worship Him in family devotion?

God can bless us only when we give Him the Christian service we owe Him as fruits for our blessings. If we do not give God *obedience*, He may have to deal with us as He did with the Jewish people. Think of the suffering they have endured. Remember the ghettos, the pogroms down through the centuries, the cremation ovens of Nazi Germany in the last war! Think of the bitter persecution that is now their lot even in this country!

Are we preaching anti-Semitism? God forbid. Anti-Semitism is undemocratic and unchristian. We owe the Jew democratic tolerance, a Christian hand of brotherhood, most of all a real effort to win him now for Christ. But I believe that God can teach us a lesson through the Jew, as a nation from which the vineyard has been removed. To whom much is given, of him shall much be required. God's chosen people rejected Christ and have thus suffered as no other nation. Let us profit from their example.

How long, then, can God bless America? First, says Jesus, as long as we give Him the fruits He desires—Christian living. And second, *as long as we build on Christ the Cornerstone.*

In our text, the Savior now drops the parable of the vineyard. This story cannot be used to present His death and resurrection. So Christ now tells the story of the "stone the builders rejected, which is become the head cornerstone."

Just as Christ was the Son and Heir to the vineyard, so He is also the Cornerstone. The building to be erected on the cornerstone was God's New Testament Church. The builders were to have been the leaders of the Old Testament Church. But when Jesus came, they rejected Him. They hacked and jabbed at God's stone and rolled it outside the city walls. Jesus did not "belong" in the religion of the Pharisees, any more than He belongs in the worldly religions of secret societies, or in the work-righteousness religion of the man on the street.

By His very rejection, Christ was made the head cornerstone. Our wounded, crucified Savior arose from the dead on the third day. Thus the rejected stone became the head of the corner in God's temple of living stones.

Perhaps you have noticed the cornerstone of a building at a cornerstone laying or simply as you have walked by. It is usually larger, and made of finer material than the other stones of the structure. On it is frequently found the date the building was constructed, and the name of the architect and contractor. The cornerstone also has more individuality and interest than the other stones, in that often a box is placed in a hollow in the top of it. In this box is placed the constitution of the organization which is erecting the edifice, a daily paper, and other items of historical interest to later generations.

But the main thing we notice about the cornerstone is that it governs every angle both in the foundation and in the building itself. The end wall is lined up with one face of the cornerstone, the side wall with the other. The vertical faces of both walls is governed by the vertical faces of the cornerstone. If the cornerstone is cut square and placed correctly, and the rest of the building matched with it, the whole building will be square, or "plumb," as carpenters say.

Anyone who has worked with buildings knows how important it is that the building be true and square. Otherwise the builders must constantly fill in some places, and cut short in others. This adds greatly to the expense of the building and detracts seriously from its appearance when completed. Nothing is ever quite right.

How thankful we can be that Jesus Christ is our cornerstone! For we who are such rough and imperfect stones can still be built on Him into His living church. Paul says to the Ephesian Christians, "You are built upon the foundation of the apostles and prophets, Christ Jesus himself being the chief cornerstone. In him the whole structure is joined together and grows into a holy temple in the Lord. In him, you also are built into it for a dwelling place of God in the Spirit."

Yes, God has made Christ the cornerstone of the Christian religion. Christ *is* Christianity. Make Him the sure foundation for your faith, and you will be saved!

Let us take heed on the other hand, to the earnest warning of Jesus, "He that falleth on this stone shall be broken." Many people aim a disdainful kick at this cornerstone that was so ostentatiously rejected by the builders. They find themselves staggering back bleeding and bruised. Not only that, but when that same stone falls upon them at the last judgment, they will be utterly crushed. They will find out, in a dreadful eternity, what it means to reject the mercy of God. These are solemn words of warning to many who do not think they need the old gospel.

I know a young man whose aged father was prevented through illness from attending his son's wedding. So the father sent a telegram, "Now another Christian home is founded, with Christ the cornerstone." Down through the years this simple benediction has inspired that young couple as they have built their family life. Homes built on the Rock cannot be shaken.

How long can God bless America? Just as long as we give God the fruits of obedience to which He has a right. Just as long as we found our nation and our homes, the strength of our nation, upon Christ the Cornerstone.

ETERNAL GOD, before whom the nations rise and pass away, continue to bless us as a nation and as individuals. Call us to repentance for the many times we have denied Thee the fruits of Christian living we should have given Thee. Help us to build our lives on Jesus Christ as the cornerstone. Hear us, as Thou hast promised to hear us, for the sake of Thy Son

AMEN

TWENTY-FIRST SUNDAY AFTER TRINITY

So Jesus came again into Cana of Galilee, where he made the water wine. And there was a certain nobleman, whose son was sick at Capernaum. When he heard that Jesus was come out of Judæa into Galilee, he went unto him, and besought him that he would come down, and heal his son: for he was at the point of death. Then said Jesus unto him, Except ye see signs and wonders, ye will not believe. The nobleman saith unto him, Sir, come down ere my child die. Jesus saith unto him, Go thy way; thy son liveth. And the man believed the word that Jesus had spoken unto him, and he went his way. And as he was now going down, his servants met him, and told him, saying, Thy son liveth. Then enquired he of them the hour when he began to amend. And they said unto him, Yesterday at the seventh hour the fever left him. So the father knew that it was at the same hour, in the which Jesus said unto him, Thy son liveth: and himself believed, and his whole house.

JOHN 4:46-53

Chapter Ten

That They Might Live

IT WAS when the busy noise of the day had been hushed into the stillness of night and the streets of old Peiping were dark, deserted lanes, that I heard a child cry. It wasn't the cry of someone suffering punishment, but the lonely cry of a lonely child, perhaps one of the many beggar children who, having no home or family, just roamed the streets, lulled to sleep at night by the dull ache of hunger and the warm flow of tears. If this had come during the busy day, it would not have been heard; for then the cries of the street vendors and the noise of the vehicles of commerce and the shuffle of many feet would have drowned it out; but now, from far off somewhere, the cry carried into my heart.

To me it wasn't just the cry of a child, but an echo of the cry of the world, when the camouflage of its sophistication and many interests has been peeled off and we hear the groan of a troubled

97

soul. Somewhere underneath humanity's crustiness it is sure to be found. Too often we are so intent on the objectives of the moment that we ignore or hurry by the aching hearts, or our many concerns make us insensible to the real needs of those about us. The world may seem a gay whirl of social events and business circles, but underneath it all is an ache that cannot be stilled. Ours is a neon-blinded society. But the ache is heard in the confines of the counsel room as troubled hearts pour out their anxieties. It is seen at the bedside when death has brought life into focus. It is felt as we stand by the grave of a loved one and learn that there are eternal verities, that a force more powerful than our own has intervened and we are helpless.

It is easy to see the world's agony written large on the rubble of cities destroyed by the crafty will of man. It is easy to see in the death toll of thousands who die of starvation because man has not been able to solve the laws of supply and demand. It is easy to see in the history of the passing of nations which rise and fall with an ever-increasing tempo. All this means little to us, however, until it affects us personally in some special way. Underneath the world's glamor is a faltering sense of security. Behind the mad rush to gain is man's sense of lack. Sometimes we have to hunt for it. Sometimes it rears its head and stares us brazenly in the face.

Not so often do we hear the cry brought to the Master, "Sir, come down e'er my child die." The world is full of remedies for everything, even for this soul agony. These are the drugs that are aimed only at deadening the pain to prevent our paying attention to the real thing. The world is full of reform, but it does not see that the problem to be solved is man himself and not his environment or the circumstances in which he finds himself. Only when man learns his helplessness does the Christian faith offer to mankind a cure for its ills; only when mankind comes to the Savior and implores His help does the Christian faith promise the cure.

It is easier to see the need of others than it is to see our own need. We can be stirred by the needs of the heathen, but we don't see the seeds of death that are sown in our own souls. It is easy to condemn the man who kills, but it is hard to recognize as murder our own neglect of the physical and spiritual well-being of others. It is easy to condemn those who are caught in the mesh of immorality; it is harder to see our own wayward thoughts as evil, or our neglect in promoting a healthy, moral community as being a sin against this command of God. It is easy to censure those who persecute Christianity; it is harder to put our neglect of the Word and Sacraments in the same category. Search yourself and you will find the ills of the world.

America is in a dangerous position. She has seen a little of the needs of the world; but having so much, she has failed to see her own real need. She is so busy with the commerce of the world, so eager for every new gadget and comfort, that communion with God is either delegated to a few paid representatives, or crowded out by pressing interests. She has so much religion, found in churches in every little village, that she has taken God's bounteous grace for granted and runs the risk of thanklessness and smugness. Something must jar her out of her complacency. Let us pray that God will not have to use suffering before we shall learn.

Jesus came to give life because "In Him was life." He is the only source of life; all other search is vain. He came that the soul which found it was hungry might be fed; He came that the soul that found it was lonely might be comforted. When men were in despair He came to give man hope. He didn't come merely to show the world how bad it was. We have a common tendency to decry the errors of our age and proclaim its hopelessness. He came as an answer to the needs, not just as enlightenment on a problem. Can the world be made to live today? Not by the efforts that are being used, for the dead cannot raise the dead; but only when the source of life is tapped can the world be resurrected to life, and it can be done.

There was no question in the mind of the official whether or not Jesus could heal his son; he wasn't looking for something spectacular. He knew that Jesus could heal the child so he came and pleaded with Jesus. Jesus' rebuke served to reveal the true faith and trust that he had. He needed that rebuke, however, lest he should put his emphasis on means rather than on results.

Can this same rebuke be applied to our work today? We talk so much of faith in God and of the power of God. We hear much talk and prayer for mass revival because we are thrilled by the numbers of "our" results. We put much emphasis on the form in which worship is to be done, or lack of form in which it must be done. We are swept with the currents of union to be thrilled by the prestige of numbers. We send missionaries to foreign lands, and when they come home are more interested in the strange customs of the people, in the numerical progress of the Church, in the little anecdotes of missionary life, than we are in the real pursuit of a soul. Are not these just surface? Aren't they just putting the emphasis on the means, on the signs and wonders again? We have fixed a mold of the Christian life and try to press everyone into it. If he can be made to fit reasonably well into this certain form, then we are quite satisfied. This has been one of the basic problems of young people's work, for we have tried to make "Christians" out of them rather than *Christians*

Or, is our world really not so bad? Does it simply need a new coat of paint, perhaps a new look? Don't expect that the non-Christian world shall see beyond this; but are *we* trying merely to renovate our world or do we want it recreated? There is only one place where that can be done, and that is in the presence of the Savior. One wonders why the official delayed for so long this coming to Jesus. Perhaps the illness was passed off as just being a "childhood disease" and not serious. Perhaps he had tried local remedies and the skill of doctors, but nothing helped. We must be aware of the true nature of the world's disease, first in ourselves, and then in all the rest of humanity, to realize what is fundamentally wrong before we really can have the cure. Coming to Christ for healing is not like coming to the doctor and informing him that we have been told we are ill, then leaving to ignore his instructions.

Is our world irretrievably bad? Is there no hope for it? To answer either yes or no is dangerous. It is as bad as an "incurable" disease, which we call incurable because we do not know the cure. Yet, to call it curable does not mean that we can put on a little salve, or take a little exercise, and it will soon be all right. How powerful is the Word of God? Can it save today? Without a question it promises the mansions of heaven to those who believe in Christ. Can the power of Christ go beyond this and save not only for eternity but save for time? Christendom must face this problem in our perplexed, warring world of today. Someone will say that the prophecies of Scripture point to the fact that there shall be wars and rumors of wars, and forget that it is said "the end is not yet." God offers a time of grace even beyond our tendency to confine and condemn. God sent Jonah to tell Nineveh that it should be destroyed, but when it repented He spared it. To say that it was eventually destroyed is to lose the point and power of the Word of God; for God has laid down an Eternal Law in Deuteronomy 30 that the nation which follows God shall live, but if it forgets Him it shall die. Don't let a false "realism" rob you of the promise of God that today we can have life, that God can make this world live.

The Christianity of today must be the prophet of God pleading with the world to turn from its wickedness and live, "for why will ye die?" Why will you pursue this way of death? It holds forth the Word of Life and says, "Hear, and your soul shall live." It goes forth conquering and to conquer. The last word of God in human affairs has not yet been spoken; He can change this world. But He must begin with me

There is, then, a Christian optimism which does not say that the world is better than it actually is, but it says that it can be better than it now is. It goes forth victoriously, apologizing for nothing in its stand, ready to meet whatever tests are before it, knowing that the all-powerful Word of the Almighty is behind it.

Go, go to work. "Why stand ye here idle all the day?" The Christian Church has not been idle. It has worked, but has the work been enough? The past has never been good enough. We dare not sit back to rely upon what has been done, or follow only in the methods that have been used. Every available means must be brought into use, and the urgency of the moment does not always permit us to say, "Give it time to test itself." As we seek ever new avenues of service, ever new opportunities to work, ever new methods to bring life to the sickened and dead body of mankind, though we seem to fail, the kingdom of God will not fail. Time will not allow us to revel in the glories of the past, or boast of the accomplishments of the present. There will come a day when the Day of Grace is ended. I cannot wait for tomorrow.

The official heard the word of Christ and he went believing. He went! Jesus invites us to come; and when we have come and heard, He sends us away, saying, "Go, and work in my vineyard." If I had a friend who was dying, and I knew a certain cure for his disease, what kind of man would I be if I didn't go and tell him; yes, not only tell him but help him; yes, not only help him but constrain him to apply the cure? For all our talk about faith, can it be that we don't believe it enough to put it to work? We spend so much on ourselves, we look out for our own welfare first, we are concerned about such trivial things in life. Can it be that we don't actually believe that Christ can cure our world today, so we settle for the best that we can get out of it? This point of view isn't radical; it is no more than men have done in other walks of life.

Today Communism stalks the world. Its disciples have a loyalty that transcends race and nation. Men have dedicated their lives for an economic theory, and their life blood is being spilled for a cause in which they firmly believe. Have we a greater cause? Have we a higher dedication? The world of the future will judge us and our faith by our actions today. "For the time has come for judgment to begin with the household of God."

In a certain place during the war a bomber crashed, and two of the crew members went back into the burning ship to bring out the badly injured radio man, who later died. They risked their lives to give a man a chance to live. Though we preach ever so forceful sermons, though we give ever so much money, though we practice our Christianity ever so well, we can never force a person to believe; but we can give him a chance to live. We can bring him to that source of life which we have found, that he may have a chance to make something of life, even if it costs us something. The cost may be greater than we expect.

"I came that they may have life and may have

it abundantly," our Master says. Now lift your eyes unto the fields and find them no longer the burned and parched fields where hope has fled, nor yet the green tender stalks where hope is nebulous. See the fields ready *now* for the harvest. God can in our world today make a new world. It may come slowly, no faster than I will become a better child of God. But God can turn the hearts of men from striving after temporal gain to seeking the treasures that can never be taken away. God can turn the hardened, warring hearts of men to hearts softened by His Spirit, hearts dedicated to the cause of an eternal kingdom in peace and service.

Is there a new and glorious day dawning for our civilization? There can be, but it will begin only when the world has come to the Master begging a word of healing, and when Christians go away believing, convinced that He can perform that which He has promised.

"And they called the blind man, saying unto him, Be of good comfort, rise; he calleth thee. . . . And Jesus said unto him, Go thy way; thy faith hath made thee whole. And immediately he received his sight, and followed Jesus in the way" (Mark 10:49, 52)

AMEN

TWENTY-FIRST SUNDAY AFTER TRINITY

The Pharisees also with the Sadducees came, and tempting desired him that he would shew them a sign from heaven. He answered and said unto them, When it is evening, ye say, It will be fair weather: for the sky is red. And in the morning, It will be foul weather to day: for the sky is red and lowring. O ye hypocrites, ye can discern the face of the sky; but can ye not discern the signs of the times? A wicked and adulterous generation seeketh after a sign; and there shall no sign be given unto it, but the sign of the prophet Jonas. And he left them, and departed.

MATTHEW 16:1-4

Chapter Eleven

A Sign for the Soul

THERE is an ancient city whose epitaph is written in the words *Deleta Silentia,* meaning "Destroyed by Silence." The legend surrounding this strange epitaph says that its prince who was once alarmed without cause, gave orders that in the future no such word of things evil was to be brought to him on pain of death. He spent his time together with his friends in days of ease and in nights of revelry. Although a dangerous foe approached the city, the sentinel dared not sound a warning. The prince was not awakened to the danger until he heard the shrieks of the dying as his palace broke into flames and the city was taken. This city came to be known as one that had been "destroyed by silence."

There are souls that impose on themselves a silence that will ultimately destroy, because they choose to ignore the signs that God has given that speak words of warning and promise of salvation.

As a rule, men are alert to the things that concern the body. They would never make the mistake of the ancient prince. When signs of danger or symptoms of sickness are evident they waste no time in giving heed. Any indication that a man's property is in a position to be destroyed by fire or by theft or by any such cause, is the sign for immediate action to avert the danger. Would that men were as ready to listen to the things that concern the soul!

A sign, whether it speak to the soul or to the body, points to the existence of something else. It has a significance and meaning entirely apart from itself. It may indicate something good or bad, something present or future. Our weather forecasts are based on signs: the winds, the barometer readings, the sky itself. Our bodies are so wonderfully made that generally there are signs pointing to good or poor health, to the presence or to the approach of sickness. Our economists can see in the ebb and flow of supply and demand, together with other factors, the rise and fall of prices. Even history has its signs that indicate a trend to good or ill. Man is wise in any particular field of knowledge in proportion as he is able to recognize and to interpret correctly the significance of the signs that God has given.

When Christ came to earth He came as the Word of God with a message to the souls of men.

When the Jews first asked of Him, "What sign showest thou unto us?" He considered it a fair question. He proceeded to work His miracles, to point out Old Testament prophecies fulfilled in Himself, to walk the way of suffering and death on the Cross and His final miracle of resurrection. All of these were signs intended to indicate the fact that He was indeed the Son of God who had authority to speak a message to the souls of men. These, together with other signs not recorded in sacred history, were given that men might believe "that Jesus is the Christ, the Son of God, and that believing they might have life in His Name."

The purpose, then, of signs is to make us aware of the presence or of the approach of that which is significant. In making us aware of such things, they are further intended to give us an opportunity to act. Signs of the approach of stormy weather have real significance to the pilot of a passenger airliner. For a pilot to be ignorant of the signs of such weather or to take off in spite of them, would be utter foolhardiness. During a recent polio epidemic there were many who had symptoms and apparent signs of that dread disease, and no one was so foolish as to ignore their significance. A provident God has given to the world of nature an abundance of signs for our well-being; in many instances we have only ourselves to blame if we have made no provision for what may befall us, for all too often we have simply ignored the signs of their approach.

Some really tragic things occur when men fail to take notice of the signs that concern their bodily lives. How much more tragic when men choose to ignore the signs that speak to the soul. Here, too, signs are given by God to make us aware of the facts of sin and of grace. "The sign of Jonah," or the fact of Christ's resurrection, was the crowning miracle in a series of signs, all intended to make men aware of the fact that the Son of God was moving among His people. The record of the gospels has the same purpose with us today. Christ the Word of God is in His Word. There we are brought face to face with Christ who presents Himself as the Savior for us to accept or to reject.

In addition to the Bible, there are other signs that point to the Savior. Our more personal experiences in life that bring us sorrow and disappointment and distress of every sort are used by the Spirit to make us aware of Him who stands ready to be "a very present help in trouble." It has been said, "When need is highest, God is nighest." This assuring fact makes every need in life a sign that points us to the scource of strength and of blessing. It is this fact that makes it possible for the Word to promise that "all things work together for good to them that love God." The burdens of life that seem to hold us down are the very means of lifting us into the heavenly places when we turn from these burdens to Him who said, "Come unto me all ye that labor and are heavy laden and I will give you rest." The very evils of this present world become signs that plead with us to save ourselves "from this crooked generation." In the risen and ever-living Christ as well as in countless other signs we have fingers that point us to a God who is close at hand with a message for the soul. This message speaks of life and salvation in the Name of Christ and becomes the star of hope to which all signs point.

The occasion of our text was the question as to what these signs should be. It would seem obvious that it is God, not man, that determines the nature of these signs. This is most certainly true in the world of nature. Even the Pharisees had learned to take note of the weather signs without seeking for other indications than these. The bodily signs of good health or ill health are not of men but of God. These are all a part of God's established laws of nature and man has generally learned to accept them as they are.

But in the realm of the soul, the Pharisee in man has led him astray into thinking that he can choose his own signs. The Pharisees came in apparent insincerity and asked for a sign even though other signs had already been given. In amazement Jesus replies, "An evil and adulterous generation seeketh after a sign; and there shall

no sign be given to it, but the sign of Jonah."
Here Christ makes it plain that it is not man's
right to claim any sign from heaven. Futhermore,
when He has given a sign, this is all they must
ask. Christ's answer has an abrupt finality to it, for
"he left them and departed."

The great botanist, Professor Asa Gray, once
asked Darwin, the great unbeliever, if he could
think of any possible proof which he would consider sufficient for faith in Christ. To this Mr.
Darwin replied, "Your question, 'what would convince me?' is a poser. If I saw an angel come down
to teach us so, and I was convinced, from others
seeing him, that I was not mad, I should believe."
To this he added, "If man were made of brass and
iron, and in no way connected with any other or-
ganism which had ever lived, I should, perhaps,
be convinced." In an attitude like this we see a
spirit common to our day. People often say they
would believe "if" they could see or hear this or
that. It all amounts to the same thing. An evil
world is asking signs of God other than those He
has decreed. To ask for others becomes only a
cloak for unbelief. Rather than look for signs of
our own choosing we should be humbly grateful
for the signs He has given.

With a note of sadness in His voice Jesus said
to the Pharisees that they "could not read the
signs of the times." They were living in the times
of the Messiah, and God had given them an

abundance of signs to indicate that fact. Had they been willing to believe or to be convinced they had more than enough evidence to bring it about. Yet they refused. Because of it we find Christ elsewhere reminding them that on the day of judgment the Ninevites would rise up to condemn them, for they repented at the preaching of Jonah, and behold a "greater than Jonah" was in their very midst. They could read the signs in the heaven, but they were blind to those signs that pointed to the Messiah.

Do we see and heed the signs of our times? We are most surely living in the time of grace, in a time when through the mercy of God we can still enter into His kingdom. The great sign of our salvation is the crucified and risen Christ. We must look for none other than this. If we are tempted like Naaman in the spirit of pride to refuse to follow such a humble way to cleansing, then we stand in danger of suffering the consequences of our own sins. The Holy Spirit is also using other signs in life to make us heed the call of the gospel. Anything that ought to lead us to reflect on the meaning of life and the destiny of man, such as sickness, loss of loved ones, suffering and burdens of every sort, are all a part of the signs by which God points men to the Savior. If we choose to live in a state of self-imposed silence concerning these things, by taking no heed, then we are making an even more serious mistake than the Pharisees and Sadducees of old. For we have nineteen centuries of Christian history and experience to add further signs pointing us to Christ.

There are other signs, too, indicating that these are the latter times. These, above all else, ought to lead us to reflect on our own inability to stand before the judgment seat of Christ. Certainly that great day when all men will be gathered before Him can not be far away. God has graciously provided the means of our salvation. There will undoubtedly be Chinese and Africans besides the Ninevites who will rise up in judgment against us if we do not believe. For mission history tells us in our day, too, of many who heeded the gospel of Christ when it was first preached to them. What excuse have we, who live in the full blaze of Christ's gospel, if we go about in unbelief finding fault with the signs by which God would point us to heaven?

When Daniel spoke to King Belshazzar concerning the mysterious handwriting on the wall, we find him more severe in his judgment than when he spoke to King Nebuchadnezzar, his father. Daniel pointed out to King Belshazzar all that happened to his father: his great and mighty kingdom, then pride of heart because of sin, then punishment through being driven into the fields as an animal until he knew and acknowledged that the most high God ruled the affairs of men. Then note Daniel's words, "And thou his son, O

Belshazzar, hast not humbled thyself, though thou knewest all this." Could anything be more evident in its condemnation? The final judgment on King Belshazzar shows him to be without excuse. The things that happened to his father were signs, had he the willing heart to read, that spoke of sin and of mercy. To the King, however, they spoke nothing whatever. Like countless others, he was "destroyed by silence."

Midnight's solemn hour will soon be tolling. These are days when man should be more and more earnest in taking heed to what concerns the soul. Thank God we have a sign for the soul, a sign that points us to Him who speaks the wondrous message of life in His name. Let us not live in the vacuum of silence where the soul must die for want of this Word of life. Let us take heed to that Sign and to all signs that speak of Him.

AMEN

TWENTY-FIRST SUNDAY AFTER TRINITY

And he spake a parable unto them to this end, that men ought always to pray, and not to faint; Saying, There was in a city a judge, which feared not God, neither regarded man: And there was a widow in that city; and she came unto him, saying, Avenge me of mine adversary. And he would not for a while: but afterward he said within himself, Though I fear not God, nor regard man; Yet because this widow troubleth me, I will avenge her, lest by her continual coming she weary me. And the Lord said, Hear what the unjust judge saith. And shall not God avenge his own elect, which cry day and night unto him, though he bear long with them? I tell you that he will avenge them speedily. Nevertheless when the Son of man cometh, shall he find faith on the earth?

LUKE 18:1-8

Chapter Twelve

The Power of Persevering Prayer

SUPPOSE that an individual or group possessed resources of wealth that could enable them to live rich and full lives. Suppose that because of ignorance or indolence they failed to use these resources, and instead carried on a meager existence. Such an individual or group would deserve both pity and rebuke. Often, however, this is the situation with Christians, because they fail to make use of the power of prayer.

> Oh, what peace we often forfeit,
> Oh, what needless pain we bear,
> All because we do not carry
> Everything to God in prayer.
> JOSEPH SCRIVEN

In our parable, Jesus speaks about prayer, the need of it, the importance of perseverance in it, and also the certainty of answer to prayer.

There is need of prayer. Prayer is not a luxury which may be conveniently passed by. It is more than a privilege. It is an absolute necessity for every true child of God. The conditions under which our lives are lived here on earth make prayer imperative. Jesus' purpose in giving the parable was to encourage prayer and perseverance in prayer. Undoubtedly He also wanted to indicate to us the need out of which prayer must come. He compares the lot of a Christian here on earth with that of a helpless widow whose very livelihood was threatened by a cruel adversary. In her own strength she was not able to protect or defend herself. Her only recourse was to plead her cause before a judge in that city.

Such, says Jesus, is the lot of the Christian here on earth, in a spiritual sense. An adversary, more powerful than we, is ever seeking to destroy us.

Have you thought deeply enough about these things to have discovered that this description of Jesus is true? The words were spoken with special reference to the times preceding His second coming, or His return in glory. They are, however, descriptive of all times. Have the onslaughts of your spiritual adversary caused you to turn to God in earnest prayer?

A recent magazine article titled, "God and the American People," refers to a recent poll conducted in the nation, and reports that 95 per cent of our people said they believe in prayer and that they actually prayed more or less frequently. Yet, the same poll brought out the fact that only 5 per cent of those who prayed reported that they ever prayed for the forgiveness of sins. In other words, the poll gave evidence of a general feeling of smugness on the part of our people, with little evidence of any sense of real spiritual need. There was little indication of any understanding of God's grace and mercy as fundamental in God's revelation of Himself or as the only foundation upon which fellowship with Him is possible. The prayers referred to must have been largely religious performances or exercises which brought certain satisfactions to those who prayed but without any definite objective or purpose.

This is not the kind of prayer referred to by Jesus. The prayer Jesus speaks of is one rising out of a real sense of need. Have such needs become real to you?

Jesus and the apostles frequently spoke of prayer as a necessity for a life in fellowship with God. It is, therefore, significant that when the apostle Paul in Ephesians 6 enjoins upon Christians to "put on the whole armour of God in order that they may be able to stand against the wiles of the devil," that he closes that section of his epistle with the words, "Praying always with all prayer and supplication in the Spirit, and watching thereunto with all perseverance and supplication."

Do you pray? Are you a praying Christian?

Our parable teaches the importance of perseverance in prayer. When this helpless widow at first came to plead her cause before the judge, he turned a deaf ear to her cry. This did not make her discouraged or cause her to give up. She returned again and again to the judge to renew her plea, "Avenge me of mine adversary." When her pleadings became more frequent and no doubt also more insistent and vehement, the wicked judge, who, according to Jesus' description of him, did not fear God or regard man, finally decided to give her redress. He did so, not because he recognized the justice of her cause, nor because he was touched by any sense of sympathy. He did so merely to save himself from further annoyance by the widow.

It seems strange, in a way, that Jesus should make use of a wicked judge to teach a lesson in prayer. The thing Jesus wishes to emphasize is the severe handicap under which the widow's pleas were presented, and the seeming hopelessness of her cause. Yet, in spite of all, she persisted until finally her pleas were heard. What an example in perseverance! So Jesus would have us persevere in our prayers even though our cause may sometimes seem hopeless.

There are times in the life of every child of God when prayer may seem vain and fruitless. What we pray for may seem indispensable to us, and our prayers may be humble and sincere. We are thinking here especially of spiritual needs, though material needs need not be excluded. Yet, even though what we pray for may seem necessary and our prayers humble and sincere, they seem to bounce back upon us as if they never reached God. In such times one is tempted to become discouraged and to give up. How comforting that Jesus has given us this parable for encouragement in situations like these!

In considering this matter of God failing to answer prayers, or at other times His delay in answering them, let us remember it is not because of any unwillingness of God to supply our true needs or any reluctance on His part to do so. God is more anxious to supply our needs than we are to seek them. However, in ignorance and short-sightedness we may pray for things which would not be good for us were they granted. James' words in 4:3 may be true of us, "Ye ask, and receive not, because ye ask amiss." We recall the apostle Paul's prayer for removal of his "thorn in the flesh," which could not be granted. Then, too, God may sometimes delay answer to our prayers in order to prepare us to receive the things we ask, as we often do in the case of children. Finally, God may delay His answer to prayer in order that He might give us something better than what we ask or think. The story of Israel in Egypt praying for deliverance while Moses was being prepared, and God's delay in answering the prayers of Zacharias and Elizabeth for a son in order that He might give them a great son who could be the forerunner of Christ, are striking examples from Scripture of delayed answers to prayer.

Jesus tells us that if the widow who had to plead her cause before a wicked and unwilling judge persevered how much more ought not we persevere who may present our petitions to a kind and loving heavenly Father who is anxious to hear us and to supply our needs. "Shall not God avenge his own elect, which cry day and night unto him, though he bear long with them?" Let not an attitude of discouragement or impatience rob us of that spirit of patience and perseverance which may make God's answer to our prayer impossible. It is such a spirit Jesus warns against in the words, "When the Son of man cometh, shall he find faith on the earth?" Jesus does not say, shall He find the church, or church activity, or even prayer. No, but shall He find *faith?* Will He find a true and living faith nourished and sustained by persevering prayer? That, according to Scripture, is the importance of prayer. It has been well expressed in a stanza from a favorite hymn by James Montgomery:

> Prayer is the Christian's vital breath,
> The Christian's native air;
> His watchword at the gates of death:
> He enters heaven with prayer.

How important that we persevere in prayer!

Finally, a few words concerning answer to prayer. Jesus gives assurance of answer to earnest and persevering prayer. He says, "I tell you that he will avenge them speedily." There may be delays owing to circumstances and conditions we cannot understand. They may be owing to conditions in our own lives or in the lives of others, as already indicated. In matters of answer to prayer we need to remember the words in Isaiah 55:9, "As the heavens are higher than the earth, so are my ways higher than your ways, and my thoughts than your thoughts."

In considering the subject of prayer many questions arise to vex us, questions which could not possibly be answered in one sermon or in several sermons. Suffice it to say here that when one considers how God has seemingly bound Himself to His children through the medium of prayer one must stand in awe before Him and marvel.

We think, for example, of how the power of prayer is shown, negatively at first, when God in Exodus 32:10 pleads with Moses, "Let me alone, that my wrath may wax hot against them [Israel] and consume them," and later on spared them because of the prayer of Moses. Or when, according to James 5:17, "Elias prayed earnestly that it might not rain: and it rained not on the earth by the space of three years and six months. And he prayed again, and the heaven gave rain and the earth brought forth her fruit."

Let it be said that prayer is not a sign of weakness, but of strength. To recognize one's own weakness and to open one's heart through prayer is to open the way to the grace and power of God.

There comes to mind a story told by the well known lay-preacher of Norway, Ludvig Hope, many years ago. A God-fearing mother was praying for a wayward son. The young man had left home and only at long intervals sent his mother information about himself. After a while he journeyed to America and then news concerning him was even less frequent. From relatives and friends there would come bits of information which increased the anxiety of the mother and caused her to be more fervent in her prayers. After a few years the mother was stricken with a lingering illness. She knew that her days were soon to be numbered. An irresistible longing to see her son again seized her. Word was sent to the son telling of his mother's wish, assuring him there were sufficient funds from her meager savings for the journey over and back, finally requesting that he try to come soon.

The young man, who by this time had become a mature man, was not at first interested in making this journey. A strange power, however, was beginning to assert itself within him which soon caused him to make the necessary preparations and to begin the journey. The voyage gave ample time for reflection. As he began to approach the shores of his homeland, memories of the past pressed themselves upon him, and he began to realize in a way he had never done before what an unworthy son he had been both to his mother and to his God.

The arrival home came a few days later. A week before, his mother had passed into the presence of her Maker and her body had been laid to rest two days prior to his arrival. Relatives and friends, however, told of a quiet joy which had filled her soul as she faced death and eternity. Though she had eagerly awaited her son's arrival and had often expressed the hope that it might not be too late, she was resigned to the Will of God and had expressed the assurance that somehow her prayers would be heard, and that she would see her son in Glory.

Tragic and sad, you say? Yes, but also comforting and glorious! For as night was settling down upon that new grave with its lonely sentinel standing by, a new day was dawning in the soul of that wayward son. The persevering prayer of a true mother had been answered!

"Lord, teach us to pray!"

AMEN

TWENTY-SECOND SUNDAY AFTER TRINITY

Therefore is the kingdom of heaven likened unto a certain king, which would take account of his servants. And when he had begun to reckon, one was brought unto him, which owed him ten thousand talents. But forasmuch as he had not to pay, his lord commanded him to be sold, and his wife, and children, and all that he had, and payment to be made. The servant therefore fell down, and worshipped him, saying, Lord, have patience with me, and I will pay thee all. Then the lord of that servant was moved with compassion, and loosed him, and forgave him the debt. But the same servant went out, and found one of his fellowservants, which owed him an hundred pence: and he laid hands on him, and took him by the throat, saying, Pay me that thou owest. And his fellowservant fell down at his feet, and besought him, saying, Have patience with me, and I will pay thee all. And he would not: but went and cast him into prison, till he should pay the debt. So when his fellowservants saw what was done, they were very sorry, and came and told unto their lord all that was done. Then his lord, after that he had called him, said unto him, O thou wicked servant, I forgave thee all that debt, because thou desiredst me: Shouldest not thou also have had compassion on thy fellowservant, even as I had pity on thee? And his lord was wroth, and delivered him to the tormentors, till he should pay all that was due unto him. So likewise shall my heavenly Father do also unto you, if ye from your hearts forgive not every one his brother their trespasses.

MATTHEW 18:23-35

Chapter Thirteen

The Grace of Forgiveness

"FORGIVE many things in others; nothing in
yourself" was the motto of an ancient Roman
poet. While we all agree with this type of philosophy, putting it into practice is another thing. Even
when we do forgive our brother, our patience all
too often reaches the breaking point. We, like
Peter, ask, "Lord, how oft shall my brother sin
against me, and I forgive him?" We forget that the
Christian stands in a middle point between mercy
received and the necessity of granting mercy. This
is one more indication of the corruption of human kind, for it is the small, vicious, sinful mind
that abounds in anger and revenge, and that is
incapable of feeling the pleasure of forgiving its
enemies.

In His inimitable way, the Master of men told
the parable of the unmerciful servant. Herein,
we see the necessity, basis, extent, and condition
of Christian forgiveness. As we read the story of

this great monarch whose wealth and power seem limitless, we are prone to excuse ourselves. This has no bearing on our personal lives. After all, we owe little or nothing, and perhaps no one owes us anything. Let us remember, however, our blessed Lord was not speaking about persons and goods in this parable; He was speaking of the relationships between individuals within the kingdom. Christ shows the discrepancy between our petitions "Forgive us our trespasses" and "As we forgive those who trespass against us."

We wonder why Jesus makes so much of forgiveness. As a matter of fact, what is there to this practice of forgiveness? An angry sea captain was once appealed to by John Wesley to forgive his man servant whom he had caught stealing. "I never forgive," was his gruff response. "Then I hope, sir," was Wesley's reply, "that you never sin." If we could stand before men and say that we are perfect, then we might well suggest that forgiveness need neither be given nor received.

Let us look at the story. Jesus must have inwardly smiled as He drew the word picture of this unmerciful servant! Here was a servant who owed the king ten thousand talents—a sum greater than the entire tax levy of Palestine. Translated into the coin of our realm, it would be the staggering figure of one million dollars. Yet the servant pleaded, "Have patience with me and I will pay you all."

But the subtle humor is not completed. The servant left the king's palace only to meet a fellow man who owed him one hundred denarii. In contrast, this debt was but one six-hundred-thousandth as much as the servant owed his king. Yet the man stood clutching his fellow man's throat as he rudely demanded, "Pay what thou owest." How impersonal we can become when we see the errors of others! This man had pleaded for mercy and received it. That wonderful experience which had snatched him and his family from doom, however, had left no glow of generosity or gratitude within his calloused soul.

The application is evident. Jesus reminds us that we can never pay God back. Our debt is great —we owe ten thousand talents; yet we, like the unmerciful servant, pledge ourselves to pay our own debts. You see, none of us has grown so much in Christ-likeness that the impulse to make restitution is not in our hearts when our consciences arouse us to our sins and shortcomings. This is true even in the face of Scripture's constant reminder that we may be able to make amends to our fellow men, but we can never make amends to God.

Our pharisaical nature immediately answers, "I'm not perfect, to be sure, but I do not owe God ten thousand talents. I have neither stolen, murdered, nor deliberately broken a moral law." That is just it! The unmerciful steward hadn't been

able to amass such a debt through open borrow-
ing, but rather through improper stewardship.
He had wasted, neglected, and misappropriated
the property placed in his care. Looking at our
lives from this point of view, we soon understand
why we owe ten thousand talents. Our sins as a
rule are not deliberate; they are sins of waste,
neglect, and mismanagement. We cut deep gashes
in men's hearts by our sharp, unbridled tongue.
We permit our minds to become cluttered with
the sordid, seamy things of life. We maintain an
outward piety while inwardly we are "ravening
wolves." We waste the precious time God gives
us. We set examples which cause the ruin of immortal souls for time and eternity. In our zeal
and our earnestness, we are neither hot nor cold.
We even have to confess that we can go for days
forgetting our God completely, neither praying
nor reading His Holy Word. This does not begin
to measure our failures in thought, word, and
deed.

Considering yourself and your relationship to
God, does your debt still seem unreasonably esti-
mated at ten thousand talents? As God opens our
eyes more completely, and we place our all at His
feet, the enormity of our debt looms before us as
a gigantic mountain whose shrouded mists can be
penetrated only by the sun of His grace.

Granted, then, that we have a debt we cannot
pay. How can satisfaction be made? According to

the teaching of Scripture, the only way that satisfaction and peace can ever come to a human heart
is by the road of repentance and forgiveness. The
Holy Spirit must bring us to the place where we
can say, "I have sinned against heaven and in thy
sight; Lord, have patience with me; forgive me."
Unfortunately, in the minds of many there exists
a misunderstanding as to the meaning of repentance. In its simplest form, repentance is turning
to God. The more we grow in Christ-likeness, the
more we will experience the pangs of remorse for
even the smallest sin. We will realize then that
we do not deserve Him, much less are we worthy
of coming to Him; but by the marvel of His grace,
we can receive Him and be forgiven. Therefore,
the call of the gospel is, "Down on your knees;
down before him in penitence and prayer."

Justice and mercy are placed side by side in the
parable. "His Lord commanded him to be sold,
and his wife and children and all that he had."
Such was the voice of justice. Then mercy came
to the fore and "the Lord released him, and forgave him the debt." Justice—that which we deserve; mercy—that which comes to us as the free
gift of God.

We do not see in the parable what it cost God
to be merciful, but the beloved John wrote, "For
God so loved the world, that he gave his only
begotten Son that whosoever believeth on him,
shall not perish, but have everlasting life." Thank

God for Calvary which has forever sealed our pardon for guilt and transgression! Thank God for the victory which He gives through Jesus Christ, His Son!

A prominent doctor in a certain community made a practice of going through his books periodically, marking certain ones, "Forgiven, unable to pay." Sometime later the doctor died and the widow felt that she and the children could use the money outstanding in these accounts. In the probate court, however, she was told she could not collect. "These accounts bear your husband's own handwriting, 'Forgiven, unable to pay.' No court of justice can go over that statement and attempt to collect."

Through the blood of Christ, God does not see our sin. He has written, "Forgiven, unable to pay" over our lives. He will forgive us all, regardless of what we have done, or of how much it will cost Him. This forgiveness is complete! "And he loosed him, and forgave him the debt"—all the debt.

Not only does forgiveness mean cleansing from sin, but also the restoration of fellowship with God. Whereas there was once a barrier between God and His child, the middle wall has now been removed. Our gracious God looks upon us "as though we have never sinned," as though His heart has never been broken, as though we have always done His will.

While the king forgave the entire debt, it was conditioned upon a similar response in the heart of the man forgiven. When this was not forthcoming, the king demanded that the servant should pay all that was due unto him. To this Jesus added these solemn words, "So, likewise shall my heavenly Father do also unto you, if ye from your hearts forgive not everyone his brother their trespasses."

This is by no means something new. We give lip service to that every day when we pray, "Forgive us our trespasses as we forgive those who trespass against us." In the words of Samuel Johnson, "Of him that hopes to be forgiven, it is required that he forgive. On this great duty eternity is suspended; and to him that refuses to practice it, the throne of mercy is inaccessible, and the Savior of the world has been born in vain."

Christianity is not a private matter between God and the individual. At the heart of Christianity is a fellowship of believers—a fellowship of forgiveness, mediated through the love of Christ. No one can say he lives unto God alone, for as he does it "unto the least of these" his brethren, he does it unto God.

What is more important, there is a reciprocal relationship between the love through which God forgives us and our forgiving love to others. The more we forgive our fellow men, the richer our own spiritual lives become, not only in the sublime joy that possesses the heart of one who forgives, but in coming to see how much God has forgiven us.

Having had some training in Christian decency, we naturally assume that we are actually practicing forgiveness. But are we? Which of us has not said, "I'll forgive, but I'll not forget"? It is "as though the God, who twice a day washes all the sands on all the shores of all the world, could not wash such memories from my mind." Forgiveness should be like a cancelled note—torn in two, and burned, so that it never can be produced against one.

This personal lesson comes to us from the parable Jesus told in days long ago. Let us sit down and check our lives against the background of our present-day living. Are we kindly considerate in public dealings and unmerciful tyrants at home? Do we expect the spirit of the law to be warped for ourselves while we apply the most stringent letter of the law to others? Do we bear resentment and ill will in our hearts toward our brothers for either actual or supposed wrong dealings? Do we expect to get even with a brother no matter what he may have done? How far are we from practicing Christian forgiveness? An honest examination reveals our failure to attain the goal.

We must act, and that immediately, to restore our broken fellowship, regardless of what it may cost us. Loss of face, or ridicule, is a small price in comparison to being cut off from God for both time and eternity. For he that refuses to forgive others tears down the only bridge by way of which he himself can ever reach heaven. But behold! The grace of forgiveness! "Forgive and ye shall be forgiven."

AMEN

TWENTY-SECOND SUNDAY AFTER TRINITY

Moreover if thy brother shall trespass against thee, go and tell him his fault between thee and him alone: if he shall hear thee, thou hast gained thy brother. But if he will not hear thee, then take with thee one or two more, that in the mouth of two or three witnesses every word may be established. And if he shall neglect to hear them, tell it unto the church: but if he neglect to hear the church, let him be unto thee as an heathen man and a publican. Verily I say unto you, Whatsoever ye shall bind on earth shall be bound in heaven: and whatsoever ye shall loose on earth shall be loosed in heaven. Again I say unto you, That if two of you shall agree on earth as touching any thing that they shall ask, it shall be done for them of my Father which is in heaven. For where two or three are gathered together in my name, there am I in the midst of them.

Then came Peter to him, and said, Lord, how oft shall my brother sin against me, and I forgive him? till seven times? Jesus saith unto him, I say not unto thee, Until seven times: but, Until seventy times seven.

MATTHEW 18:15-22

Chapter Fourteen

The Christian's Duty
Toward an Erring Brother

NO ONE understood the weaknesses of His disciples better than Jesus Himself. No one was more deeply pained and grieved when troubles beset them. No one so earnestly desired that their love for one another should be pure and holy, and their fellowship peaceful and blessed, as His prayer indicates:

"Father, I pray for them which thou hast given me, that they may be one, even as we are one" (John 17:9, 11). It is for this reason He has given them the instruction contained in this gospel text. He exhorts them to be ruled in all their relations by the law of forgiveness, and especially in their conduct toward erring brethren, by the spirit of brotherly love.

Forgiveness and brotherly love should be a living fact in the life of every Christian. Therefore, the theme selected for our consideration is "The Christian's Duty Toward an Erring Brother." He should be willing to forgive without measure or limit, and also to reprove in the spirit of love.

"Then came Peter to him, and said, Lord, how oft shall my brother sin against me, and I forgive him? till seven times? Jesus saith unto him, I say not unto thee, Until seven times: but until seventy times seven." There is to be no limit to forgiveness. The limitless character of forgiveness springs from its divine origin. Forgiveness is God-given and, therefore, God-like. It belongs to the ethics of heaven. It cannot be enforced in the law courts on earth. Forgiveness is above law as the sovereign who pardons in clemency is above the judge who is compelled to condemn in justice.

God forgives without limit. He requires, of course, the condition of repentance, and this we have a right to demand also. When repentance is present, He forgives, no matter how hardened the offenders may be, who have grieved His Spirit many a time before. It is only the limitless forgiveness of God that makes it possible for us to be pardoned by Him. Then it is incumbent on us to show the same spirit toward our fellow men.

One thing, however, the Christian does not always remember, which is hard for him to learn, and which needs to be refreshed in his mind, and re-affirmed in his conscience all the days of his life: his willingness to forgive must *know no end,* his readiness to pardon must know no bounds, and his duty is to forgive "not seven times, but seventy times seven."

It was not that Peter was unwilling to forgive, nor that he was slow to do so, that prompted his question to the Savior. He thought, however, there ought to be a limit to forgiving. Jesus makes it plain that forgiveness is not a matter of mere numbers, or quantity, but it is something deeply spiritual. So long as your love is limited by rules of arithmetic, so long as you are able to count your brother's offenses, and the times you have forgiven, you have really not forgotten what has passed between you and your brother, nor grasped the inward spirit and meaning of forgiveness.

When love begins to count, it also begins to die. David declares that God counts our tears, and Jesus informs us that our Father in heaven has numbered the hairs of our heads. But of the sins that are forgiven, He keeps no count. *They are entirely blotted out.* If you live a life of meekness and humility before God, if you have need of a Savior who will not reckon your sins against you, you must also practice a love that forgives others without counting the times.

This deep truth Jesus proceeds to impress upon the minds and hearts of the disciples in the parable which immediately follows our text, that of the unmerciful servant. Just as God's forgiveness

toward us is boundless and unceasing, so, too, ours
should be toward our fellow men. Here Jesus is
our shining example. As Jesus, so His follower.
We receive forgiveness from Jesus; we grant forgiveness like Him. It is the same forgiveness,
Christ's forgiveness, working through us on others.
If we do not forgive like Jesus, then we have not
accepted forgiveness from Him. "If ye forgive not,
neither will your heavenly Father forgive you."
What Jesus has done for me is to be my rule of
life. Will that be your rule of life, too?

The joy of receiving forgiveness from Jesus is
the joy of a sinner, the joy of giving forgiveness
like Jesus is the joy of a saint. The one is earthly,
the other heavenly.

Out of the last war comes an illustration of the
spirit of Christian forgiveness. A young German
soldier killed an English soldier, also very young,
in battle. In his pocket he found the name of his
mother back in England. The German wrote to
her and told what had happened, and said that
because he was a Christian he was writing to ask
her forgiveness for killing her son. Immediately
the mother wrote back and said that she, too, was
a Christian and, therefore, she was glad to forgive. Then in her letter she invited him to come
to England after the war would end and to be her
son. Surely the spirit of forgiveness is a wonderful
spirit. It is God-given.

What Jesus practiced Himself, He preached to

others. "First be reconciled to thy brother, and then come and offer thy gift" on the altar to God (Matt. 5:24). This is not a mild advice, it is not only a suggestion. This is the Lord's absolute and unconditional command. How terribly in earnest the Lord is may be seen from the fearful penalty appended, "Agree with thine adversary quickly . . . lest at any time . . . thou be cast into prison. Verily, I say unto thee, Thou shalt by no means come out thence, till thou hast paid the uttermost farthing" (Matt. 5:25, 26).

By repetition Jesus impresses that duty upon the hearts of Christians. In the parable the unmerciful servant lost all the great forgiveness of the Lord because he refused to forgive a little debt to a fellow servant, and so he was delivered to the tormentors. "So likewise shall my heavenly Father do also unto you, if ye from your hearts forgive not every one his brother their trespasses" (Matt. 18:35).

If Jesus never tires of hearing our daily prayer, "Forgive us our trespasses," though we come with it again and again all the days of our life, should there be any hesitation or unwillingness on our part to reach out the hand of forgiveness to our brother, who asks to be reconciled, though he comes seven times a day?

Shall we then do nothing to stop the wrong? Indeed we shall. "If thy brother shall trespass against thee, go and tell him his fault between thee and him alone." That is Christ's method for you to stop the wrong, the only method open to you in all this wide world. You must be willing to forgive without measure or limit, but it is also your duty to reprove in the spirit of love.

Does Jesus mean that we are to close our eyes to our brother's faults, to gloss over his sin, to condone it and conduct ourselves toward him as if he had not sinned? Not at all. For the duty of forgiving does not preclude the duty of reproving him in love. Thereby do we show him that we truly love him, when we thus seek to win him from the consequences and service of sin, for the kingdom of God. Jesus says in our text, "If thy brother shall trespass against thee, go and tell him his fault between thee and him alone." He says also in another place, "If thy brother trespass against thee, rebuke him." Of course, his sin must be real, not fancied; open, not secret; proven, not merely suspected. "Brethren, if a man be overtaken in a fault, ye which are spiritual, restore such an one in the spirit of meekness; considering thyself, lest thou also be tempted" (Gal. 6:1). That this is one of the most difficult of Christian duties is true and, therefore, it is a duty often grossly neglected by many Christians. For that reason it becomes all the more necessary to call attention to it. "Thou shalt in any wise rebuke thy neighbor, and not suffer sin upon him" (Leviticus 19:17). Solomon says, "Rebuke a wise man and he will love thee." A greater man than Solomon, our Savior, has said, "If thy brother trespass against thee, go and tell him his fault." St. Paul directs, "Reprove, rebuke, exhort with all long suffering." These are but a few of many similar passages of Scripture that might be cited to show that to reprove an erring fellow Christian is the command of the Lord. This is every Christian's duty, and it is your duty, too.

It will not do to say, "Let the pastor do it, or let those do it who are better qualified than I am." It is indeed the pastor's duty. It is also the duty of those better qualified than yourself. But first of all *it is your duty*. The pastor cannot be everywhere. He cannot see everything, and that question of qualification is indeed a delicate one. The truth is that those who think themselves qualified and, therefore, use impertinent boldness, are generally not qualified for effectual brotherly admonition. If a brother has sinned against you, or you see a brother in danger of losing his soul through error and sin, then let not the feeling of disqualification seal your lips. Pray God to open your lips to speak a word of instruction, rebuke, or comfort, as seems needed.

The apostle says, "Ye which are spiritual restore such an one." If you are spiritual, if you are a Christian, it is your duty to apply brotherly admonition. Do you think it is right for any one of us to shift this duty to the shoulders of others?

Remember, this matter of Christian reproof is a serious matter, a duty which the Lord Jesus has plainly and strongly enjoined upon us to perform. "Go and tell him his fault between thee and him alone." In a Christian's life we find that Christ expects both the offended and the offender to be seeking each other. But do not wait for him to come to you. Show him plainly how he has wronged you, and how he has offended God. This should be done in private, gently, kindly, and in love. Such a treatment may win your brother, while public rebuke, open denouncements might only incense and harden him.

We are to see the offending brother alone. This is the last thing some people will do. In pride or in fear, they shun the very person they should seek. They refuse to speak to him. Often they spread the tale among their neighbors, how they have been wronged by their brother, and how he has failed in many things. A train of gossip is started that causes much harm and bitterness. Let us seek out the person who has wronged us and who has also sinned against God, and let us be open and frank with him. Often a little quiet talk will bring about a mutual understanding and "thou hast gained thy brother." Fail to warn him of the spiritual danger he is in, neglect to caution and reprove him, if you see him sinking in sin, and you become partaker of his guilt; aye, God will require his blood at your hands.

In reproving an offending brother, we must make it clear that it is his eternal welfare we are seeking. It must be obvious that we have no personal dislike nor feeling of vengeance. It should be made manifest to him that we do it from a sincere conviction of duty and a loving Christian heart. What a power and influence there will be in reproof when administered in such kind and sympathetic spirit! It should melt and reclaim anything but a heart of adamant.

Reproof will require wisdom. There are moods, and places, and seasons. Christian tact will be keen to distinguish which are opportune, and will not endanger its hopes by coming in "an undue season." What can be more calculated to win him than telling him "his fault between thee and him alone"? Surely that should disarm him of the thought that you came to humiliate him or seek reparation. It should assure him of your entire good faith and friendship. Moreover, privacy will promote the frankness so necessary to an understanding. If the admonition is administered face to face in proper season with humility of spirit, it can scarcely fail of its purpose. If he hears you, you have gained your brother for yourself as a friend—above all, for the kingdom of God.

Much Christian patience will be needed. You may not be successful in your first approach to the brother who has sinned against you. It will probably be necessary to repeat your visit to him for this important cause. If after several attempts to win the erring brother privately—for you will continue as long as there is hope to see him alone—it may be wise to proceed to the next step. Call in one or two other Christians. This is also to be private. To avoid unnecessary publicity the smallest number is called in. The gravity of their advice may convince the offending brother that he is in the wrong. He may listen to the pleadings of these disinterested persons and be persuaded. These witnesses have the double function of seeing also that the reproof is administered in the spirit of love and humility, and that to reject it the reproved would be found impenitent and impossible.

If this process fails, we are to bring him before the congregation, that by its united impact of love upon him, its suasion and prayer, he may yet be won. He must needs be a hardened offender indeed if he can withstand the alliance of such prayer, for it has the promise, "If two of you shall agree on earth as touching any thing that they shall ask, it shall be done for them of my Father which is in heaven."

If all these efforts under God fail, "let him be unto you as an heathen man and a publican," cut off from the blessings and privileges of the congregation. He is no longer to be acknowledged as belonging to the fellowship of saints, according to the power of the keys, "Whatsoever ye shall bind on earth shall be bound in heaven." After all, he has really excommunicated himself.

Yet, he is not lost forever. There is still hope that he may be won. Where the discipline of the Church ceases, its mission work commences. Even the last step has been taken with the object of saving him. The purpose of all church discipline is repentance, conversion, and everlasting salvation.

How wonderful it would be if we Christians would follow the instruction given by the Lord Jesus Christ in our text. The followers of Jesus would then really become the salt of the earth and the light of the world. Our Church would become a mighty power, going forward in faith and life and activity.

Therefore, dear Christian friend, when in the walks of life, in relations of the home, of the congregation, of the school, in the intercourse of social and business life—for it is there men most often sin against each other—you find it difficult to forgive without measure or limit and to reprove in the spirit of love, turn to Jesus Christ. From Him you will receive the power to do as He did who said, "Father, forgive them, for they know not what they do." "As Christ forgave you, so also do ye."

AMEN

TWENTY-SECOND SUNDAY AFTER TRINITY

And he said unto them, Is a candle brought to be put under a bushel, or under a bed? and not to be set on a candlestick? For there is nothing hid, which shall not be manifested; neither was any thing kept secret, but that it should come abroad. If any man have ears to hear, let him hear. And he said unto them, Take heed what ye hear: with what measure ye mete, it shall be measured to you: and unto you that hear shall more be given. For he that hath, to him shall be given: and he that hath not, from him shall be taken even that which he hath.

MARK 4:21-25

A great responsibility rests upon the hearers of God's Word. The Savior teaches here by parables and figurative expressions that those who receive His gifts and graces become "candles" or "lights" that are not to be hid, but to shine. We are to use what we receive to the glory of God and the benefit of others. If we do not *use*, we *lose* what we have. That is God's law. Gifts and graces will rust for want of wearing.

The source of such radiant living is Christ. "They looked unto him and were radiant" (R.V., Ps. 34:5). Life is conditioned upon light. The Almighty Maker of heaven and earth first commanded, "Let there be light: and there was light" (Gen. 1:3). Since then, He who upholds the universe by the power of His mighty Word has wisely directed the course of the sun, moon, and stars to give light to the dwellers upon the earth. But He who created light for our physical well-being did not withhold the light to illumine the soul. The promise of the Messiah and Deliverer was given first to our fallen parent in the garden. The prophets pointed forward to the coming "Light of the world." Isaiah proclaimed, "Arise, shine; for thy light is come, and the glory of the Lord is risen upon thee" (Isa. 60:1). John the Baptist came to bear witness of that *Light*. He was not the Light himself, he declared, but he was sent to bear witness of Him that people might believe on Him. He pointed to Him and declared, "Behold

trance of thy words giveth light" (Ps. 119:130),
and "Thy word is a lamp unto my feet and a light
unto my path" (Ps. 119:105). The darkness of sin
has settled all around us. "And this is the condemnation that light has come into the world, and
men loved darkness rather than light, because
their deeds were evil" (John 3:19). As an army
chaplain, I saw an example of this when I visited
the Dachau horror concentration camp twelve
miles from Munich. A Polish soldier who had
spent three years there told me about it. He said
that a thousand prisoners were crowded into each
barrack. It seemed almost unbelievable. He first
showed me the old crematorium which dated back
to 1933 where Hitler sent his own people who
opposed him. The new crematorium was built in
1940. It happened that coal was hard to obtain
for cremation purposes so mass burials were often
conducted outside the city. The guide said that
shortly before someone was killed or expected to
die from brutal mistreatment or starvation, letters
were written to nearest of kin stating that the
prisoner was going to be removed to a much nicer
place. Upon cremation another letter followed the
ashes, regretting that such a one died before the
move was made possible. Next to the cremation
room was a gas chamber. Prisoners were given a
towel and a bar of soap and told to go in there
for a shower. Only dummy showers were found
in this room. Two hundred were crowded in each

time, and then the gas turned on. There was an opening about a foot square through which the SS troops would watch the agony of the dying and determine when they were dead. Other brutalities too horrible to describe were committed here to the 213,000 people who went through this camp. Himmler had ordered the place evacuated and more mass killings as the American army was pressing in, but our tanks rolled in before this was accomplished and found the evidence.

It was horrifying to see with what exactness, scientific precision, and utter inhumanness this thing was carried on by highly educated and civilized people. The only writing I saw was a plaque in the cremation room stating, *"Cleanliness is our watchword; be sure to wash your hands."* Oh, the irony of it all! That gave me an insight into the cold, inhuman, and atrocious Nazi mind. Paul describes this graphically when he says, "Their throat is an open sepulchre; With their tongues they have used deceit; The poison of asps is under their lips: Whose mouth is full of cursing and bitterness: Their feet are swift to shed blood; Destruction and misery are in their ways; And the way of peace have they not known: There is no fear of God before their eyes" (Rom. 3:13-18). How true are the words of our text, "For there is nothing hid, which shall not be manifested; neither was anything kept secret, but that it should come abroad."

Let us not forget that though we have not stooped to such atrocities, our hearts are deceitful. "All have sinned and come short of the glory of God" (Rom. 3:23), and it is possible to be refined, moral, and good and still live in sin and love darkness more than light. God requires repentance of sin, and stepping out into the light. He has hung many beautiful lamps in the universe —His glorious sun to shine by day and the beautiful moon and stars to shine by night. He has, however, given us the most glorious light to illumine our souls—His Word, which is a Saving Light—a light to shine upon the road that leads to the Lamb. It is a blessed Word for Christ comes to us clothed in this Word. He is "The Light of Life" (John 8:12), and by faith in Him each one of us can say, "The Lord is my light and my salvation" (Ps. 27:1).

A few years ago we visited Wind Cave in the Black Hills. A guide led us, but we also needed lights, so lanterns were carried. In one of the large rooms of the cave all of us sat down while the guide lectured to us. Then we were all asked to extinguish our lanterns to experience how dark utter darkness is. It was really dark down there hundreds of feet underground with no possibility of daylight filtering in. What utter darkness in our lives without the "Light of Life," Jesus Christ, shining in us and through us by means of His Word! The Word of God becomes a guide to lead

us step by step. It is also a Light that we must
use diligently and prayerfully. The more we use
it the more light it gives us. The darker it is, the
brighter the Light shines.

The lights are the believers. Jesus says, "I am
the light of the world" (John 8:12), but He also
says, "Ye are the light of the world" (Matt. 5:14).
"The entrance of thy words giveth light" (Ps.
119:130). Therefore, we are to be lightbearers.

The scientists tell us that we do not get light as
direct beams from the sun, but we have light by
diffusion. The sun shines upon the dust particles
in the air, and they diffuse the light. Each dust
particle becomes sort of a miniature sun to send
out the light in all directions. The Church is
Christ's great golden candlestick (Rev. 1:20), and
your particular church is one of its branches. You
and I are to be "candles" on that branch, lit by
the Father of Lights through the "Sun of righteousness" (Mal. 4:2). The church father Augustine said, "Christians are the Light lighted; Christ
is the Light lighting."

The purpose of light is to shine. We are to shine
from the candlestick. We are not to hide our lights
under the bushel. Your "bushel" may be some
friend; it may be your business; it may be your
love for pleasure; it may be greed, lust, selfishness
or indifference. Most of us sin greatly in disobey-
ing Christ's command to us to let our light shine.
We are desperately afraid of offending others. As

our light becomes conspicuous there will be some who will admire, commend, rejoice and imitate. There will be others who will envy, hate, censure, and rebuke. Why should we be afraid of these? The sun shines just as brightly behind the clouds. We must be sure to shine to illuminate others, not self. We are to set Christ forth, not ourselves. After all, we have no light in ourselves. What we have is received from Christ. We are just reflectors of His light. The evangelist Moody said, "Light-houses don't ring bells and fire cannons; they just shine, that's all." The command of Christ is clear, and that is to let our light shine. He has given us His gospel light so we can proclaim Him to the world. He has commanded it; He expects it; He punishes us if we neglect it. "With what measure ye mete, it shall be measured unto you." In other words, if you shine, God will shine through you. If you hide your light, it will gradually be extinguished. If you do not use what you have, you will lose what you have. If you bury your talent, you betray your trust in Him. This is an inevitable law in the realm of human knowledge, and it is just as inevitable in the spiritual realm.

The prophet looking ahead said, "Arise, shine for thy light is come, and the glory of the Lord is risen upon thee" (Isa. 60:1). We also hear the Psalmist say, "Let the redeemed of the Lord say so" (Ps. 107:2). Jesus Himself declares, "Go home to thy friends and tell them how great things the

Lord has done unto thee" (Mark 5:19). Again He commands, "Go ye into all the world and preach the gospel" (Mark 16:15). We need this divine enthusiasm. The shining Christian is the radiant Christian. The shining Christian is the strong and growing Christian.

Where are you to shine? Right where you are. What better place than your own home? Let the world see that your home is one of light and love. Are mother, father and all the children Christian in your home? Another place to let your light shine is in the church. Here is the best place for fellowship, worship, warmth, and encouragement. We must also let our light shine in our community and state. The Samaritan woman when she had found Christ went back to her village and invited all its citizens out to see and hear the Savior of the world, and many believed on Him because of her testimony. Paul declares that every Christian is "an epistle known and read of all men" (II Cor. 3:2).

Dr. C. J. Sodergren says that at the best we are like "barn lanterns" used in earlier days—rusty, cracked and smoky. They were not ornamental or bright, but the small flame did give enough light to see to do chores, and for the members of the family it was a sign of life and activity in the night. There were some things that could be done to get the best light from the lantern. Oil in it was an absolute necessity; the wick could be trimmed, and the chimney kept bright and clean. We need to keep our lamps trimmed and burning bright. We need to watch that life of ours so that it is kept pure and holy; we need to do those deeds of self-sacrifice for others; we need to keep ourselves busy lighting other lights. We are asked to turn many to righteousness and we shall shine as the stars forever and ever (Dan. 12:3). Let us take the torch of salvation and hold it high these days so many may see Christ and be saved.

AMEN

TWENTY-THIRD SUNDAY AFTER TRINITY

Then went the Pharisees, and took counsel how they might entangle him in his talk. And they sent out unto him their disciples with the Herodians, saying, Master, we know that thou art true, and teachest the way of God in truth, neither carest thou for any man: for thou regardest not the person of men. Tell us therefore, What thinkest thou? Is it lawful to give tribute unto Cæsar, or not? But Jesus perceived their wickedness, and said, Why tempt ye me, ye hypocrites? Shew me the tribute money. And they brought unto him a penny. And he saith unto them, Whose is this image and superscription? They say unto him, Cæsar's. Then saith he unto them, Render therefore unto Cæsar the things which are Cæsar's; and unto God the things that are God's. When they had heard these words, they marvelled, and left him, and went their way.

MATTHEW 22:15-22

Chapter Sixteen

A Christian's Allegiance

STANDING at attention, we have often spoken the words, "I pledge allegiance to the flag, to the republic for which it stands, one nation, indivisible, with liberty and justice for all." Remembering that ungodly, unbelieving men may sometimes rule, that any nation may engage in unjust wars, that politics is a dirty game and corruption is to be found in every state, can Christians make that pledge? Can the believer in Jesus Christ swear allegiance, his eyes on the flag, his hand on his heart? The question needs to be answered, and every believer ought to be at peace with his conscience in this vital matter. A man is made, his destiny determined, and his life's course charted by his loyalties.

Jesus comes to grips with it in our text under conditions no easier than those which face His followers today. Proud Rome ruled the tiny nation

God had called His chosen people. Roman soldiers marched in the streets of the Holy City. Tax collectors everywhere demanded tribute money. All of this conspired to set the stage for the enemies of Jesus to put Him in a role which they were sure would discredit Him. They had set an ingenious snare; they were certain He could not escape this time. If He said that it was lawful to give tribute to Caesar, the violently patriotic Jews would undoubtedly stone Him. If He said that it was unlawful to pay tribute, Roman rulers would mete out swift judgment upon an insurrectionist. Jesus gave an answer, however, which not only defeated the intentions of His enemies but which throws the light of divine wisdom clearly upon the whole matter of the Christian's allegiance. "Render therefore unto Caesar the things that are Caesar's and unto God the things that are God's."

"Render unto Caesar the things that are Caesar's." Give back to the state those things which are its due. The Christian is to be loyal to his country.

The political-religious situation which Jesus faced was quite involved. Roman rule had, on the whole, been quite satisfactory, but according to the law Caesar was to be worshipped. Religions sanctioned by the state were immoral and debasing. In Palestine the Herodians were politically active, seeking the advancement of the House of Herod. The Pharisees were strict adherents of the theocratic ideals of Judaism. They believed that any king not a Jew was no proper ruler for them according to Deut. 17:15, "Thou mayest not set a stranger over thee." The cross currents of loyalty and conviction which played upon the situation therefore made a clear and specific pronouncement extremely hazardous. Yet, Jesus called for the tribute money. He drew from His enemies an unwilling admission of their bondage. Then He said, "Render therefore unto Caesar the things that are Caesar's." Since Rome rules and you are in bondage, pay to Caesar those things due unto him.

In his Epistles, the apostle Paul instructs Christians to be in subjection to rulers and to pray for them. In Rom. 13:1-7 he gives them at least two reasons for being loyal to their country. First, there is no power but of God; the powers that be are ordained of God. The Pharisees were right. The present state of affairs was not God's original intention. In fact, God planned to rule Israel even without a king and selected one only because Israel repudiated His best plan for them. The monarchy was God's second best plan. Then when the kings led the people into flagrant disobedience and open rebellion against Him, God had to send bondage as the third best plan for governing the chosen people. They were in servitude because they had sinned and their very sufferings were designed to lead them to true repentance and

faith. The powers that ruled Israel were there because God had permitted and ordained them as
the best possible solution to the problem of governing a people which had proved itself incapable of God's better plans. Therefore, it was
right to render unto Caesar the things that were
Caesar's.

Paul states his second reason for loyalty to country in these words, "For he is a minister to thee
for good." The state preserves law and order.
It provides schools, road and communication sys-
tems, police and fire protection, flood and erosion
control, public works projects and a host of other
things through which government is a minister
unto men for good. They ought, therefore, to
render unto Caesar, to recognize the benefits received.

What does it mean to us as present-day Christians when Jesus says, "Render therefore unto
Caesar the things that are Caesar's"? It means that
we as citizens are to love our country as ordained
and given to us by God. We are to exercise our
citizenship, always seeking to make our country
a place where righteousness dwells, remembering
that "righteousness exalteth a nation but sin is a
reproach to any people." As individuals we are
to be active in government, shaping its policies,
guiding the course of its history by the Christian
principles of honesty, integrity, and unselfishness
which can best aid our country in serving God's

purpose among us. As voters, as office holders, as taxpayers, as magistrates, as governors, as presidents, Christians are to take their stand for every measure that will serve the common good and against every subversive, immoral cause in government. Too often because of the risks, the dubious honors, the meager rewards, Christians have withdrawn from their civic responsibilities. They have paid their taxes, but they haven't rendered unto Caesar the things that are Caesar's. All too frequently they have allowed unprincipled, destructive, greedy groups to rule the city, the state, or the nation. They have been content to sit by and criticize, often not even exercising their democratic privilege at the polls. Christians need to exercise their faith and to apply it to the society in which they live. They must, by their fearless unselfishness, disprove the statement of the English philosopher Hobbs when he says, "The only motive for human conduct is selfishness."

Dr. Walter Judd said in a conversation recently, "More Christians are needed in public office who will dare to be statesmen rather than politicians, who will work tirelessly for the common good of all men everywhere." Every country desperately needs men and women who will brave the hazards and bear the responsibilities of public office, citizens who will apply their Christian faith in every issue which confronts them.

Martin Luther and his contemporaries recognized the Christian's obligation to the state and elaborated upon it in Article XVI of the Augsburg confession: "Of Civil Affairs, they teach, that lawful civil ordinances are good works of God, and that it is right for Christians to bear civil office, to sit as judges, to determine matters by the Imperial and other existing laws, to award just punishments, to engage in just wars, to serve as soldiers, to make legal contracts, to hold property, to make oath when required by the magistrates, to marry, to be given in marriage. They condemn the Anabaptists who forbid these civil offices to Christians. They condemn also those who do not place the perfection of the Gospel in the fear of God and in faith, but in forsaking civil offices: for the Gospel teaches an eternal righteousness of the heart. Meanwhile, it does not destroy the State or the family, but especially requires their preservation as ordinances of God, and in such ordinances the exercise of charity. Therefore, Christians are necessarily bound to obey their own magistrates and laws, save only when commanded to sin, for then they ought to obey God rather than men (Acts 5:29)."

Christians should be loyal to their country because the powers that be are ordained of God and rulers are ministers unto them for good. "Render therefore unto Caesar the things that are Caesar's." But as Scripture indicates, there is a point at which allegiance to country is to be definitely submerged to the supreme allegiance which the believer owes to God. The Christian recognizes his duty to be a loyal citizen, but he never forgets that his citizenship is in heaven. He fears and obeys God rather than men. He renders unto God the things that are God's. He may lay loyalty, love, liberal participation in the affairs of the state, yes, even life itself on the altar for his country, but always his supreme allegiance is to the God who made him, redeemed him in Jesus Christ, and gives him daily all blessings, including those which are his as a citizen of a certain country. Whenever there are conflicting loyalties, he chooses God first, last, and always. No other loyalty compares to that which rises out of the love which God has awakened in the believer's heart, a deep, abiding, exalting, sanctifying allegiance to the King of that kingdom which shall never pass away. When allegiance to God comes into conflict with allegiance to Caesar, Christian martyrs are made. In apostolic times believers died by the thousands because they would not deny Christ and worship Caesar. In World War II, Martin Niemoeller, Eivind Berggrav, and Kai Munck took the same stand. They were ready to die rather than to compromise their faith. Kai Munck knew that his life was at stake when he said, "To stand silent in the face of deeds of sin is to speak the language of the devil."

In every land Christians must choose the supreme loyalty, giving their allegiance to God and His kingdom. Karl Barth analyzed the situation of the church under the Third Reich and his conclusions clearly indicate the higher allegiance which must be ours in whatever country we live. "Speaking generally, the church has not to be at the service of mankind, and so, not to the German people. The German Evangelical Church is the church with reference to the German people; she is only in service to the Word of God. It is God's will and work, if by means of His Word mankind, and of course the German people, are ministered unto. The church believes in the divine institution of the State as the guardian and administrator of public law and order. But she does not believe in any State, therefore, not even in the German one and therefore not even in the form of the National Socialist State. The church preaches the Gospel in all the Kingdoms of this world."

It is disturbing to read in the article "God and the American People," by Lincoln Barnett that most of the American people put material or political allegiances above religious convictions. This means that there is an open door in America for the very worship of the State which destroyed Germany and Italy and today engulfs Russia. Christians are to be loyal to their country, but they must never forget that their supreme allegiance is to God. They are to practice the advice

of Augustine, "Give the money unto Caesar, thyself unto God."

The denarius, the tax penny, had Caesar's
image and superscription reminding everyone who
saw it that he lived under the dominion and rule
of Rome. Christians see in all men the image of
God. They remember "In the image of God created he them." They read God's inscription upon
every living soul, "I have redeemed thee, thou
art mine." Believers understand that kingdoms
may rise and fall, civilizations may come and go
but God extends day by day that kingdom which
shall endure when the heavens shall be rolled up
like a scroll and the earth shall vanish away. The
believer's supreme allegiance is indicated by the
great apostle when he says, "For our citizenship
is in heaven; whence also we wait for a Savior, the
Lord Jesus Christ; who shall fashion anew the
body of our humiliation that it may be conformed
to the body of his glory, according to the working
whereby he is able even to subject all things unto
himself" (Phil. 3:20-21).

The believer in the Lord Jesus Christ can
pledge his allegiance to the flag of his country,
recognizing that the government is a part of that
God-ordained framework under which his life is
to be lived. He is not to condone or strengthen
evil men or purposes, but rather as a Christian
to exercise his faith as a citizen so that his nation,
a power ordained of God and a minister unto him

for good, may realize the Christian ideals as far as possible. When the reins of government are seized by wicked men who demand of the believer a denial of his faith, the Christian is ready to die rather than submit. His supreme loyalty requires him always to render unto God the things that are God's. Recognizing always his duty to his country, working for its welfare, taking his place as a citizen, paying gladly his tribute to Caesar, the Christian's higher allegiance to God, the constant desire of his heart, is expressed in Kingo's hymn:

On my heart imprint Thine image,
Blessed Jesus, King of Grace,
That life's riches, cares, and pleasures,
Have no power Thee to efface;
This the superscription be:
Jesus, crucified for me,
Is my life, my hope's foundation,
And my glory and salvation.

AMEN

TWENTY-THIRD SUNDAY AFTER TRINITY

And Jesus sat over against the treasury, and beheld how the people cast money into the treasury: and many that were rich cast in much. And there came a certain poor widow, and she threw in two mites, which make a farthing. And he called unto him his disciples, and saith unto them, Verily I say unto you, That this poor widow hath cast more in, than all they which have cast into the treasury: For all they did cast in of their abundance; but she of her want did cast in all that she had, even all her living.

MARK 12:41-44

had taken place in the soul of this poor widow. Her husband had died and left her no inheritance. Life had been severe and bitter. She had to earn her living by hard work. It was difficult to make both ends meet. She had to learn to get along without all those things that belong to the comforts of life. There were times that life seemed like a blind alley. It was then that she learned to look up and ask God to come into her life and take over where she had failed. It was a hard thing to do, because she knew that she had failed Him so often. Perhaps she had failed to go to the temple to worship because she had nothing to offer. It may be that she had failed to trust in Him, and had even cursed the lot that was hers. Why did God take away her husband? Why did He leave her to struggle alone in the world where no one seemed to care or be concerned about a lonely widow? All this made it hard to look up. Pride had often ruled in her heart, and pride always has a way of closing the door to God. Finally, there came the time when there was no other way but up, and she implored the merciful God to come into her life and help her. No cry of a lost soul ever goes unheeded at the throne of grace. God heard. He always hears the cry of the penitent. He hears. He answers prayers. He did in the life of this poor widow. She found her way to the temple. There was no longer the struggle within her soul whether she should go or whether she should not, even though what she had to offer was little. Our text pictures her as she gives her offering in the temple.

We read the story of our text and are likely to think that Christ's sole interest was in the money received for the temple tax. We see the outward act of the offering but fail to see beyond the gift. We may see the giver, the widow, yet forget that beyond her was the Giver—the Giver of Life, the One who made such an offering possible. Christian stewardship must first of all be Christian. Christian giving is not a cause but an effect. It is the result of something that has been experienced, the personal experience of God's abounding grace through Christ.

We are disturbed about the fact that in this day of high salaries and large incomes the Church is receiving but a small percentage of the income of its members. We find it difficult to understand that the per capita contribution was proportionately higher during the depression than during this period of prosperity. The answer is obvious. To use the words of our text, much of the giving today is "of their superfluity," that is, from their abundance. Often it is a giving that still trusts in the security of materialism. It is really giving from a surplus or overage, and therefore is not an act of faith.

From the Summary Report of the Lutheran World Federation Assembly at Lund, Sweden, we read, "Christian stewardship is 'the practice of the Christian religion' on the part of those who have been won for Christ. It is man's response, his total response, to God's grace." Christian giving, then, is an act of faith based upon an act of grace. It is God's grace as revealed in the redemption of His Son, Jesus Christ. It rests upon the premise of ownership, "Ye are not your own; for ye are bought with a price." Though tithing is a convenient and commendable plan for giving, God did not redeem just one-tenth of us and therefore has a right to only one-tenth. God redeemed the whole man for time and eternity and, therefore, has a just claim upon the whole man, his time, his talents, and his means. As Christians we love because He loved us first, even so, as Christians we give because "God so loved the world that he gave"—gave His only begotten Son for us. The reason we are disappointed in the stewardship of the Church is that we separate Christian giving from Christian living. Frankly, they are synonymous. They are one and inseparable. Christian living is Christian giving, and by that same token Christian giving is Christian living. Of the widow we read she gave "even all her living."

Before this widow of our text had arrived at the point where she could, with a boldness of faith, give her last two mites in the offering at the temple, she had learned to place herself completely into the keeping of God who could and would provide for her far better than all the money man can accumulate. That is consecration; it is trusting in the Divine Security of Him who in the Scriptures has said over five hundred times, "fear not." It is simply trusting in the eternal promises that are found on nearly every page of Holy Writ. It seems so simple, so logical; and yet it is one of the most difficult lessons we learn. Some never learn it. When that lesson is learned, then the Church's problem of stewardship is solved. The whole question of stewardship becomes a question of consecration. It is not only a question of ownership but also one of possession. We all belong to Him by virtue of Calvary and the ransom price that was paid there. But do we yield to Him the possession of our life? If we do, then we are in His care and keeping and know that, "My God shall supply every need of yours according to his riches in glory in Christ Jesus." Living in that Divine Security we learn the secret of the widow "who did cast in all that she had, even all her living."

AMEN

Chapter Eighteen

Those Unprescribed
Decisions

THE strangest miracle Jesus ever performed, I think, was the one where He arranged to have a temple tax paid with a piece of money that He promised would be found in the mouth of a fish. Even so, the miracle is of secondary importance. Our attention is drawn to His reason for paying the tax.

He really didn't have to pay that tax. As He intimated, He was a son of the temple and sons of the temple were free of such responsibility. Actually, no one really had to pay it, it was a voluntary contribution which adult Jews customarily paid each year. Since it was customary, there were some who apparently wondered if Jesus regularly paid it, and so asked Peter. There may have been some underlying motive of hostility in the question, but it may as easily have been a casual inquiry such as anybody might put to a church member, "By the way, does your pastor contribute to your church?"

That isn't an unusual question either, for people sometimes wonder just what is the general practice of pastors. Opinions differ as to whether a pastor should or should not be expected to use offering envelopes. One man who has been a church trustee said to me once that he thought it was rather silly for a pastor to give money to the treasury from which his salary came in the first place. Others are quite insistent that a pastor should take his place among the congregation's contributors if only for the sake of setting an example. Certainly there is no ecclesiastical rule to which one must conform.

Well, there you have an illustration of what brought into the New Testament the account of Jesus paying the temple tax. The incident lives on and takes a prominent place in our Christian thinking because of what Jesus said as He announced His decision, "Sons are free. However, not to give offense. . . ." His decision was made only after considering the consequences of His action to other people.

There appear to be situations in life when decisions cannot be arrived at by referring to a rule or regulation. How well we know that! Those difficult questions about conduct—how we frantically search for the chapter and verse which will tell us what to do. It has made some people wish almost desperately for instructions as complete and as detailed as the instructions given for the building of Solomon's temple. Young people especially do that, and some of them are inclined to be impatient with what appears to be indecision or uncertainty in pastors or leaders. "Isn't the Bible supposed to tell us what is right and wrong?" they demand of leaders.

The luckless leader who has that question put to him is in a difficult spot. If he says the Bible doesn't tell us in all instances the right and wrong of some things, he is suspected of undermining confidence in the Bible as the Word of God. On the other hand, if he seeks to explain how the Bible teaches us to distinguish evil from good he finds himself involved in a discussion in which someone sooner or later comes up with the observation, "It's all in the way you look at it." Biblical support for any proposed decision is met with the remark that the Bible has to be interpreted and "It's all a matter of interpretation."

Then someone bolder than the others but speaking their thoughts will say something like this, "You would think that if the Bible is supposed to be the Word of God it would tell us plainly what we are supposed to do and not leave so much up to individual interpretation."

The discussion struggles on. It's the kind of thinking and talking you might expect to find only in the United States where we place so much confidence in rules and laws and by-laws. We are well trained to say when people do not act as they should that "there ought to be a law."

But they had laws in the days of Jesus, too, and the same confidence in minute regulations—not least in their religious writings. Every aspect of life was presumably covered by the Torah, other writings, and by the teachings of the scribes and Pharisees. They covered everything in detail, even prescribing the width of the border of garments to be worn in order to express the degree of a man's religion. On the whole, these regulations were accepted by the people, with a moderate amount of debate, of course.

It is always easy to accept the idea of following regulations, for it seems to bring religion down to practical simplicity and it makes it possible for a person to act in a way that relieves him of personal responsibility. We like that! They liked it also in biblical times as exposed by Jesus in His Sermon on the Mount and on other occasions.

In the great sermon He repeatedly used the expression, "Ye have heard it said," wherein He referred to the letter of the laws which they followed more or less with ease since it was done mechanically. "But I say unto you," said Jesus as He directed attention to the spirit of the laws, thus drawing distinction between conduct and character.

Something like that prompted Jesus on another occasion to pronounce one of His severest rebukes, saying, "Woe to you, scribes and Pharisees, hypocrites! For you are like whitewashed tombs which outwardly appear beautiful but within they are full of dead men's bones and all uncleanness. So you also outwardly appear righteous to men, but within you are full of hypocrisy and iniquity."

Scribes and Pharisees are separated from us by many centuries now and would not have to be mentioned except that they represent the age-old inclination to dress up the outside of self by following the accepted rules with only secondary concern for one's real self. It is out of this inclination that we get the religious thinking and activity we call legalism.

Legalism is one of those "church-words" we hear frequently without fully understanding its meaning. The general impression is that it is something bad, so no one would ever admit to being a legalist. When called upon to define it, however, some follow the course of a vacation school teacher I once had who asked the pupils if they knew what jealousy meant. We didn't know so he tried to tell us, but got no further than saying, "It's something bad; we should never be jealous." That didn't help us to understand how God could be jealous which was a subject we also studied.

So legalism is bad! But what is it? Why is it

bad? It is the tendency to settle all matters of Christian conduct by referring to a rule or regulation which frequently is but a custom or tradition. It is bad because it originates in the general belief that a person is a Christian if he does so and so and refrains from doing such and such, and it gives the impression that that is the nature of Christianity. It is false theology, for it actually originates in an attitude or belief which may be expressed about like this, "If God will give us the directions we'll do the job of being Christians—with some help from Him from time to time over the rough places."

That is ridiculous, of course! It is as though a monkey were to say, "Teach me how and I will be a human being."

When we start complaining that the Bible does not give us clear enough instructions in how to be Christians we are acting like monkeys who complain in monkey language that they cannot be human beings because the human beings do not teach them clearly enough!

We should know that the miracle of the gospel is not that it teaches men how to act like children of God (although that would be a miracle of a sort) but that it *creates* children of God of people who by nature are not His children. "That which is flesh is flesh," said Jesus. Except we be born again we cannot see the kingdom of God.

The upsurge of joy which so frequently characterizes conversion comes not because the convert has been given new instructions on how to act like a child of God but because he has been told that he can quit the game of pretending to be one.

That is really Good News to the person who has begun to suspect that even other people may have caught on to his play-acting, not to mention his certainty that if there is a God He must surely have long since seen the man behind the mask. All men play at it. Christians are those who have discovered it does not count in eternity. It is a solemn fact that the conduct of even the best Christians is never entirely free of pretense. The people we think of as saintly are no exception, although in all probability they spend more time in penitential prayer than the average Christian, which is one reason why they are saintly.

Incidentally, when people make the charge that the church is full of hypocrites, they are right in the sense that no one in the church is everything he appears to be. But they fail to take into account that many of the people in the church know better than their fellow men what they themselves are, and therefore are seeking forgiveness and strength. The man who is really a liar is the one who loudly boasts, "At least I am not a hypocrite!" Man's pretenses may protect his reputation, but no pretense to goodness can ever make one a child of God. Only God can do that in the new birth.

When people start insinuating among themselves that some essential instruction has been left out of the Word of God, it is well that they determine why they want clearer instruction. If it is because they think with clearer instruction in conduct it would be easier to become the children of God they are definitely on the wrong track. Any one of the commandments by itself is sufficient to reveal our failure. Increasing the number of commandments or instructions only piles up the evidence that convicts us.

Mark Twain must have understood that as he said, "It isn't what I don't understand in the Bible that bothers me, it's what I do understand." St. Paul in a more evangelical way declared the same fact when he wrote, "If it had not been for the law I should not have known sin. I should not have known what it is to covet if the law had not said, Thou shalt not covet" (Romans 7:7). Add any new rule to a person's life and you probably have added something with which his inner nature is disposed to argue.

Wait a minute now! This is not to say that ignorance of the law of God is spiritual bliss. Increasing the evidence of sin does not increase the sin, much less does the introduction of law produce sin. You cannot equate recognition with derivation. Identification of a germ does not produce the disease. While it is true that man often rebels more vehemently when he is confronted with a law, the law cannot be said to have produced his capacity for vehement rebellion. It has only exposed it.

So the purpose of the argument up to this point is to show that any desire for greater clarity in biblical directions, if it is because we think it would make it easier to be Christians, is a vain desire. With the law comes only the knowledge of sin. While it is ultimately good for us to have that knowledge it does not make it easier to live as Christians. Christian living becomes a pleasant experience only when we realize that our life in God is by grace, not by works.

"I have been crucified with Christ," said Paul; "it is no longer I who live, but Christ who lives in me; and the life I now live in the flesh I live by faith in the Son of God, who loved me and gave himself for me." "If justification were through the law," Paul continues, "then Christ died to no purpose."

When people in a discussion group start complaining about lack of directions in conduct or when charges are made that someone surely cannot be a Christian because he does such and so, I am inclined to paraphrase for them Paul's words to the Galatians, "O foolish people! Who has fooled you into this kind of religious thinking? Tell me this, did you receive the Spirit of God by obeying commandments and laws or did you get it as a gift? Are you so foolish? Having begun with the

Spirit, are you now thinking that the rest is up to you? Does he who supplies the Spirit to you and works miracles among you do so by the works of the law, or by hearing with faith?"

There is a place, nevertheless, for instruction in Christian living as indicated by Jesus when He said, "The Counselor, the Holy Spirit, whom the Father will send in my name, he will teach you all things." "For," He said, "he who has my commandments and keeps them, he it is who loves me." One who loves Christ will permit the Holy Spirit not only to bring to remembrance the commandments of God as they apply to daily living but he will permit the Spirit so to take possession of him that those decisions for which there can be no specific commandment will be made with consideration of its possible consequence to others.

Christians are like the individual members of a body, as Paul tells us. Some of their activity can be clearly directed and defined, but there are some activities which can be determined only with regard for the coordinated activity of the whole body. The hand which persists in being the limb for walking, if one can imagine such a thing, will harm the entire body. The Christian who persists in living independently with no consideration for the effect on others will harm the whole body of Christians and other people.

That is the implication of Jesus' action in paying the temple tax. Personally He was free of any

obligation to pay it. In due consideration of consequences of His action to others, however, He
chose to pay. In so doing He only ran the risk,
so to speak, of having people misunderstand or
consider Him foolish. Not paying the tax would
have done real harm. Just how, I don't know.
Suffice it to say that Jesus saw the possibility of a
real hurt and determined His action accordingly.

Some of our decisions as Christians must be
made in the same fashion. There are actions which
can do no more than unintentionally cause misunderstanding. Other things can be the occasion
for doing spiritual and irreparable harm. No
Christian dares to be indifferent to those possibilities but needs to be sensitive to what can cause
real hurt, what can only be misunderstood, and
how to distinguish one from the other.

I knew a man once who considered neckties a
sinful adornment and not to be worn. Should a
Christian refrain, therefore, from wearing a tie
in his presence? It is an illustrative incident. What
a Christian should do would have to be determined only after due consideration had been
given to consequences. So he could reason this
way: since one can hardly ascribe any moral quality to a tie and since it does not seem possible
that one could do more than cause misunderstanding, there would be no reason for removing the
tie. On the other hand, deciding not to wear a
tie would probably encourage the false belief that

Christianity and tie-wearing are incompatible. Worse yet, it would contribute to the false belief that you can identify a Christian by whether or not he wears a tie. This brings us right back to where we are suggesting that if God will give us the detailed instructions we will proceed to be Christians. Play-acting again.

By the way, there is yet another possibility of doing damage in such a situation. The Christian who, for instance, chooses to wear his necktie may do so with self-conscious pride that he is a more intelligent Christian than the one who feels he should not wear one. He may go even farther, as some have done in similar situations, and deliberately flap his tie in the other person's face to show that he isn't bothered by such silly ideas. Flaunted freedom can be as damaging as ill-considered decisions.

We need Spirit-guided thinking. No book, not even the Bible in a new edition every day, could cover all situations in life. But Spirit-led consideration of consequences to other members of the body of which we are a part will prepare the Christian for the decisions that must be made. Our mistakes we must leave with God in the confidence that He will not only forgive us but may even turn our failures to good results. God, make us sensitive to the needs of other members of the Body of Christ!

AMEN

TWENTY-FOURTH SUNDAY AFTER TRINITY

While he spake these things unto them, behold, there came a certain ruler, and worshipped him, saying, My daughter is even now dead: but come and lay thy hand upon her, and she shall live. And Jesus arose, and followed him, and so did his disciples.

And, behold, a woman, which was diseased with an issue of blood twelve years, came behind him, and touched the hem of his garment: For she said within herself, If I may but touch his garment, I shall be whole. But Jesus turned him about, and when he saw her, he said, Daughter, be of good comfort; thy faith hath made thee whole. And the woman was made whole from that hour. And when Jesus came into the ruler's house, and saw the minstrels and the people making a noise, He said unto them, Give place: for the maid is not dead, but sleepeth. And they laughed him to scorn. But when the people were put forth, he went in, and took her by the hand, and the maid arose. And the fame hereof went abroad into all that land.

MATTHEW 9:18-26

Chapter Nineteen

The Faith for Our Day

THERE are silent forces in this world and they seem strangely able to work miracles. The warmth and light of the sun make vegetation grow and the power of gravitation draws everything to the center of the earth, holds the universe together and keeps us from flying out into space. In the realm of the spiritual a vision of but a moment's duration will transform a wastrel into a devoted servant of God and an experience of love will change a giddy girl into a consecrated mother who will count it a joy to make a thousand sacrifices every day for the family God gave her.

In our text it is the silent force of faith—faith in Christ. We are intrigued as we see it strangely resident in the hearts of both the ruler of the synagogue and the friendless woman who supplicate the help of Christ. Quiet as the evening hush and winsome as a child's smile, it had the gift to bring them the fulfillment of the deepest longing they had ever known and even more. So natural is it in its simplicity that it would seem to be within the reach of all. Certainly it is the faith we need in our day.

We note regarding the faith of both the suppliants in our text the spirit of expectancy. Here is the plea of the officer of the synagogue: "My child is even now dead but come and lay thy hand upon her and she shall live." It need not trouble us that in their recital of this incident both Mark and Luke state that the ruler came to Jesus first of all when his daughter was "at the point of death" and that the word of her actual demise came to them along the way. There is a place called "at the point of death" that is as far beyond any human power to help as is the place of death itself. Jairus' faith in Jesus to heal his daughter when she was "at the point of death" became the faith that believed He could restore her to life when death had actually come, even though it needed a little encouragement.

The burning faith of the woman is uniquely described in her own words, "If I may but touch his garment I shall be made whole." It was her conviction that if she could but press her way through the crowd, timidly come from behind and with the tip of her finger touch the extreme border of the flowing robe of Jesus that she would be well again. What expectant faith both of these had! You never hear of anything like it outside of the Christian religion. Only the God revealed by Jesus can inspire a faith so buoyant and daring.

We know that expectancy is an important element in faith, or maybe we should say that it is the very essence of it. "Faith is the substance of things hoped for, the evidence of things not seen." Where there is no expectancy there is no faith, but where there is true faith there is expectancy. You can determine the genuineness of your faith by the measure of hopefulness there is to be found in it.

Anyone who traveled in post-war Europe knows that the people in those countries suffered. Not only had their cities been bombed but their economy and even their spirits had been bombed, disrupted, shattered! The burden of their inquiry was always this, "Do you think America will come to our aid?" The thing that interests us about that now is that they expected something from us. We liked it, whatever our politics may have been. It did something to our national ego.

Everybody wants to be wanted and to feel that they have a place to fill and a work to do. You expect something of other people, and they expect something of you. That is the joy of living. The whole fabric of civilization is woven out of the faith that people have in one another. It is so in the kingdom of God. Christ wants us to look to Him in faith. It makes Him happy when we do and we can never expect too much. "Ye have not because ye ask not."

We observe not only expectancy as the nature of faith but victory as the result of it. Both petitioners of our text received what they so earnestly sought. The father was given his daughter back from the limbo of death and the wasted woman was made whole.

We often find ourselves wondering about the miracles Jesus performed in His earthly ministry. Not only the number of them, even though He seemed literally to pour out blessings upon the people, but we think of the nature of those miracles. He made the blind to see, the deaf to hear, the lame to walk; He healed the sick and raised the dead. On the shore of the Sea of Galilee He fed the five thousand with five loaves and two small fishes. To other multitudes He gave health and life and limb. These were all physical and material miracles. Not that Christ bestowed only such blessings even then, but in the general picture of His earthly works they do seem to abound.

There was a reason for this. Christ taught two great truths while here on earth: He was the Son of God. He must be crucified and rise again.

The works He performed were intended to establish His claims regarding His Person and the purpose of His coming. If He could miraculously feed the multitudes with bread when He was here on earth, why was He not the One who centuries before had fed the wandering Israelites with manna from on high? If He could heal the incurably sick, why then could He not also forgive sin? If He could recall a soul from the abode of the dead, did He not then have life in Himself and hold the secret of life eternal? These were only logical deductions. Jesus meant them to be such and thus to the doubting He flung this plea, "Believe me for the very works' sake." If His works could bring people to believe in Him for what He really was and could do, He could give them the greater blessings of heart and salvation.

Such are the gifts He bestows in this dispensation of the Holy Spirit. Not that He does not still give lesser blessings, but the spiritual and eternal do abound. Here is a young couple who have an only child and he is taken ill. They are told his case is incurable. For months they watch over him and see his body waste away under the blight of disease. They turn to Jesus in their sorrow but they are to receive something they never sought. They were not given their boy back to health but they were to make a discovery. They found the Lord. They learned that with Him there is mercy, that there is a life beyond, that their boy would grow up in heaven and that they could all meet again in the Home Eternal. They were really happy in this thought. This was a far greater gift both to the parents and their boy than if he had been given back to life here.

Jesus Christ is as good and generous as in days gone by. Miracles are still being performed. Their number is even greater. "Ask and ye shall receive." If you do not get what you immediately seek, be sure that you will receive what you more sorely need.

In our text we observe that the expectant faith Christ honors with His gifts is for all people to have. There is something in the story that tells us that. We read that "the fame hereof went abroad into all the land." The reason these acts of mercy spread the fame of Jesus was that they declared that new hope had come for everybody.

Sorrows and disappointments of various sorts come to all hearts. The unhappy Jairus and the disheartened woman had no priority on the knowledge of either the person or power of Christ that they should find help. As a matter of fact, they lacked the gospel narratives and the story of Christian experience over the centuries as we have them. In the light of all that they lacked it would seem strange that they could believe at all. Moreover, whatever formal religious training they may have had only helped to account for the superstition that was in their faith.

But the factors that always make for true faith were present in them. They were conscious of a deep need that was beyond their power to remedy. Under God their hearts were yielded and out of the little that they heard about Christ and felt, the Holy Spirit created a true faith even though it was not perfect. It has often happened that some who have had but a smattering of Christian knowledge come into a living faith, while others who may have basked all their lives in the full light of the gospel never come into any personal experience. Thank God for any tragedy in your life that threatens to black out the joy of living. A ray of hope will break through and it comes from Him who is the light and hope of all.

The ways in which people come to Christ have their background in an endless variety of circumstances. There is an instance of a light-hearted couple who spent their Sundays traveling. If they visited relatives who went to church they would go along with them but beyond that the church and her message meant little. They found their interest and pleasures elsewhere. They did, however, join a church. Why not? After all they had been "brought up" in the church. Then you should have heard the story they had to tell sometime later. Not only had they joined a church but they discovered something unexpected there and found joy in Christian service. They would not think of missing a service on Sunday. It was more thrilling than anything they had ever known! As they told their story a strange light would cross their faces and you sensed that an inner and satisfying experience had come to them.

What had happened? The thing that had hap-

pened to this couple was that they had discovered
that Christ was for them also to possess and enjoy.
He is not for a selected few. He is for everybody.
He is for you, too. *For this cause* He came.

The expectant faith that Christ honors and offers freely to all is the great need of the world
today. "At the point of death"—"my child is even
now dead." "Suffered much"—"spent all she had"
—"nothing bettered"—"rather grew worse." These
cryptic words used by Matthew, Mark, and Luke
to describe the despair of the synagogue ruler and
the distraught woman of our text can also be said
to describe the situation in the world today. Certainly conditions have greatly worsened. Scientists
warn us that civilization is "at the point of death."

There is hope for the world even today, however. That is the confidence that comes to us out
of the text. Jairus, a man of honor, position, and
prestige, had used every means at his disposal to
save the life of his darling girl but now he stood
hopeless. The woman, once wealthy but having
spent all in a futile effort to regain her health, was
now not only penniless but wasted and worsened.
From the depth of their misery these two, un-
known to each other, look for help and then it is
that they spy Him.

It is to Christ that the world must turn for
peace and security. All the devices of statescraft
have utterly failed to save mankind and now we
are faced with an impending global catastrophe.

But Jesus Christ is the Son of God and is able to save all mankind. "O Jerusalem, Jerusalem, how often would I have gathered thy children together but ye would not." Thus Christ spoke to His chosen people and thus He offers the only hope remaining to all the world, and it is a sure hope.

The way to bring Christ to the world is indicated in our text. Jesus left the disputation of the Pharisees in the house of Matthew and went in ready response to the plea of the officer of the synagogue. We should like to have seen the look in the faces of the Pharisees after Jesus had healed the doomed woman, brought the ruler's daughter back from the dead, and to have heard His reassuring words in those baffling moments. We wonder what they really thought! The works of Jesus could not be gainsaid, and here was the secret for the success of His Word in the world.

Christ has taught us that not in disputation and argument is the world saved, but in the worship and work of the Church. Therefore has God set aside a day each week for worship. Therefore also has He ordered the Church to "go out and make disciples of all nations." There is nothing more telling upon the world than the devotion of God's people to the cause of His kingdom. We are convinced that if only the children of God had attended faithfully upon the worship in His House on the Lord's Day and rendered Him dutiful service, the world would have been spared the trag-

edies of two global wars and the consequent present threat to all civilization. After the cessation of
hostilities in World War II, President Truman
called upon the churches to take the lead in the
recovery program. The Word of God and the
prayers and sacrifices of His people can make the
kingdoms of the world the kingdom of our Lord.
There are those who will scorn this thought as
Jesus was scorned when He would raise Jairus'
daughter from the dead. Christians know better.
There is One greater than the atomic bomb, and
He is the Son of God, the Savior of mankind. We
do not need a new world but we need a new point
of view.

The most effective billboard sign we have ever
seen was one in Germany in 1935. Why it impressed us so, we shall probably never know. Here
is the text of it: "O Germany, Hear the Word
of God!" How different it would have been if not
only Germany but if other nations as well had
"heard the Word of God"! Of all people, Christians should be interested in their nation and in
the world. Christ was. He was a true patriot, the
first real internationalist and served a world-wide
cause. Note these passages: "Behold the Lamb of
God that taketh away the sin of the world." "God
gave His only begotten Son" because "He so loved
the world." To be like her Lord, the Church must
take a global view of life.

The expectant faith that Christ recognizes and

offers to all is not only the need of humanity but also the need of each individual. The family of mankind is made up of individuals, and it is as such that we must all live and struggle and choose our lot. The problems of the world are problems within each one of us. Jairus may have been the ruler of the synagogue, but it was as a father that he had to meet his sorrow. The woman of our text may have had her circle of wealthy friends, but in the misery of her prolonged illness she lived alone.

The Savior of the world is the Savior of the individual, your Savior and mine. He loves the world because He loves each person. He has redeemed mankind because He has redeemed each individual. He is a specialist in the problems of your life. If you yield to His Spirit and earnestly seek Him, He will give pardon, strength, comfort and hope.

I once heard a preacher raise the question as to what is the greatest thought in the Bible. He proceeded immediately to answer the question by saying that the greatest thought is the resurrection of Christ. He who rose from the grave the third day, who called the daughter of Jairus back to life and healed the hapless woman who flicked the border of His garment—that Christ is sufficient for all your needs. He is the Son of God and in Him is life eternal.

AMEN

TWENTY-FOURTH SUNDAY AFTER TRINITY

All that the Father giveth me shall come to me; and him that cometh to me I will in no wise cast out. For I came down from heaven, not to do mine own will, but the will of him that sent me. And this is the Father's will which hath sent me, that of all which he hath given me I should lose nothing, but should raise it up again at the last day. And this is the will of him that sent me, that every one which seeth the Son, and believeth on him, may have everlasting life: and I will raise him up at the last day.

JOHN 6:37-40

Chapter Twenty

The Charter of Christianity

THE world is constantly flaunting before us invitations to buy things, to try various remedies for human ills, to join something, or to go somewhere. Whether we read our papers and magazines, turn on the radio, or walk the streets, it is the same story.

A national soap advertisement tells us their product does everything in the family wash. Another advertisement urges us to "Try our remedy for fast relief from pain," or to "Enroll in our course and become a success." Whether you are afflicted with arthritis, fallen arches, or falling hair, there will be plenty of people who will urge upon you their remedies with a reckless promise of success.

But whatever human panaceas you try, you are faced with the possibility of failure. There is one invitation and only one upon which we can depend, one which will not fail us whatever our need. It was issued by Christ in our text, "He that comes to me I will in no wise cast out."

Only our Heavenly Father knows how many souls down through the years have grasped this promise of Christ and have as a result been carried safely through guilt, through temptation, and death. We who counsel with people on spiritual problems can testify that we have used this passage many times in dealing with troubled souls. We have witnessed not infrequently how it has brought peace to fainting spirits. It constitutes a standing challenge to men.

This proclamation of Christ, if we may call it such, follows several wonderful events recorded in this sixth chapter of John. Jesus had fed the five thousand with five barley loaves and two small fishes, and had reminded them that He was the Bread of Life. Then follows the miracle of Jesus walking on the sea. The attention of the multitudes was aroused as a result of these miracles and the gracious words of Life that fell from His lips. In spite of all this, however, many continued in their unbelief.

Jesus was not discouraged. The greater the unbelief, the sweeter the words that came from His lips. Notwithstanding the unbelief He had encountered, He utters the glorious words which have given hope and courage to all approaching Him throughout the centuries. "He that comes to me I will in no wise cast out." Is not this sublime truth the very heart of Christianity? It is a truth as potent and as firm today as when Christ first uttered it.

This word is an explanation of what true Christianity is. As we carefully read the text, we see a picture of Christ standing in the midst of a world's need, in the midst of sinful men with all their heartaches, suffering, and tragedy. As Jesus compassionately surveys this need, He reminds us that He has the answer to all men's problems, that He is both able and willing to provide all the help needed. Is not this essentially the burden of Christianity's message? We do well to remember that the center of Christianity is Christ, Christ alone. He is the Alpha and the Omega, the first and the last, the beginning and the end. He has the Keys of Death and of Hades. He is the way to life eternal. What the sun means to plant life, Christ means to the soul of man. Without the sun, plants must die. Without Christ, man cannot live. If Christ be not in our hearts, we are children of death. Christ is the center of the Christian message. He is the center of our prayers, our hymns, our liturgy and our sermons. A sermon that fails to exalt Christ as Lord is spiritually empty and meaningless.

Consider further how Christ challenges man in our text. "He that cometh to me." We are reminded that "coming" is the way of salvation.

Christ went to Calvary's cross to open the way for man to God. Had there been another way for God to save men, He would undoubtedly not have given up His only begotten Son to die on the cross. The way to everlasting life is not through Socrates, Aristotle, Plato, Will Durant, not via Harvard or Yale, but over the road stained by the blood of Jesus that was shed for the remission of sins. This road is the only way to God. Jesus said, "No man comes to the Father but by me."

One colored gentleman was a little bewildered by the way of salvation as presented by his pastor. He remarked, "What am he sayin', dat preacher man? Show me da road!" Surely Christ has given to him and to all of us a simple and clear answer in the truth of our text.

To be saved means to come to Christ. But what is "coming"? Jesus had performed many miracles, restored sight to the blind, unstopped deaf ears, and even raised the dead. Great crowds had followed Him. They had witnessed His power, had heard the life-giving messages that He uttered, but many did not come to Him. As Jesus issued the proclamation of our text, He was perhaps thinking of the many who still were unbelievers in spite of all they had seen and heard. So He casts out the net again with an appealing message of great simplicity, inviting and encouraging sinners to come to Him that they might be saved and kept. "He that comes to me, I will in no wise cast out."

"Come to me" is Christ's challenge to men. If you would be saved and kept, "Come to Christ." Perhaps the colored gentleman we mentioned would press us further to clarify the question, "What do you mean by the phrase 'Come to Jesus'?" How do we come to Him?

To "come to Jesus" means, first of all, that we must approach Him with submissive trust, to commit ourselves to Him as Lord and Savior. It means that I yield Him my heart, accepting Him as He claims to be.

A certain lad was asked to define saving faith. He replied, "It is grasping Christ with the heart." No theological definition has put it more accurately. We do well to think of faith not only as trust but a coming to Jesus. Surely the one who grasps Christ with the heart comes to Him. What a challenge to sin-bound and weary hearts. What an encouragement to troubled and anxious souls. Above the tumult, the agony, and travail of men sounds the call of Christ, "Come to me."

In coming to Jesus, we do well to remember that He invites us to come just as we are. Consider again the words of a familiar hymn:

> Just as I am without one plea
> But that Thy blood was shed for me,
> And that Thou bid'st me come to Thee,
> O Lamb of God, I come!
>
> CHARLOTTE ELLIOTT

It is indeed true that we haven't a single plea of merit to offer Christ except this that we have been redeemed by His blood. In His name and with the plea "Jesus died for me" we can boldly approach the throne of grace. Do not wait to come to Jesus until you feel you are fit to come. There is nothing you can do to cleanse your heart to prepare yourself for that meeting with Christ. You may have your questions. You may ask, for example, "How can the holy and pure Christ receive me, an unholy and impure creature?" That is the glory of Christianity, that Christ receiveth sinful man. It was Spurgeon who once wrote:

> Let not conscience make you linger,
> Nor of fitness fondly dream;
> All the fitness He requireth
> Is to feel your need of Him.

That last line suggests our next thought, that in coming to Christ we should come with a sense of need in our hearts. We all need Jesus. The thief, the murderer, the adulterer, the gossip, the Sabbath breaker, the selfish, the proud, the haughty—all need Jesus. To all Jesus says, "Come unto me." It matters not who you are or where you are. It matters not as to blood or nationality. It matters not whether you are rich or poor, famous or obscure, young or old. It matters not if your sins are as scarlet. It matters not whether you are an unfaithful husband or wife, a youth whose footsteps have begun to wander, or an aged person

who has become a backslider. It may be a corrupt
politician, it may be a soul who breathes threaten-
ings, slaughter, and harm to God's children—no
matter, He invites you, "Come unto me." I can
find no exception to this invitation. Whosoever
will may come, and He that comes will not be
rejected. Listen to this gracious word—you who
have broken your vows, whose solemn promises at
Confirmation to be true to God "even unto the
end" have not keen kept. Listen to this word, you
who are living in secret sins, you whose love for
God and His Church has cooled. He says to you,
"Come unto me."

Come with a sense of need, knowing that you
are a sinner, knowing you need His forgiveness
and cleansing. Come to Jesus confessing your sin
and your need of mercy, and He will point you to
"Calvary's holy mountain" where you may wash
and be clean. Is your conscience accusing you?
Come to Him! Is your load heavy? Come to Him!
You have tried the broken cisterns of the world
and you are still thirsty. Come to Him who said,
"He that believeth on me shall never thirst."

One of the great human problems is that of
sickness and pain. Thousands of people are sick
every day. Our mental hospitals all over this country are filled. One doctor states, "It is quite likely
that hereafter one in every twenty-two persons
born in the state will go to an institution for mental disorder." It is evident that people in increas-

ing numbers are breaking in their minds under the stress and strain of our high pressured life today. Ask any doctor, and he will tell you of the increasing numbers of people who are suffering from heart trouble, high blood pressure, and a variety of forms of nervous trouble.

In spite of all gadgets and appliances designed to make life easier and happier, in spite of all the luxuries and amusements which abound in the average life today, it is evident that man is not happier, but that he is restless. Somehow life fails to satisfy him. There is the stress of inner conflicts, of frustration and its consequent nervous tension. A great many people are sick from worry. These people—the physically sick and the mentally ill—need the cooling balm and the healing grace of Jesus Christ. Nerves must be quieted if our bodies and minds are to be healed. An inner peace must replace the worry, the inner conflicts and tensions.

Perhaps you are struggling with the problem of fear. I dare say more people are wrestling with that problem than ever before.

No class of people is exempt from fear. People everywhere have fears of themselves, fears of others, fears for the future of the world in this atomic age, fears of sickness, poverty and of death. But Jesus says, "Come to me." When we do, He speaks His reassuring word, "Fear not, I am the first and the last, and the living one; and I was dead and behold, I am alive forever more, and I have the keys of death and of hades" (Rev. 1:17-18). "Fear not" are words of Christ to all struggling with the problem of fear. "I am with you, I have all power, I will help you to conquer fear," is His message to us. With Jesus, we can be unafraid of life, death, or eternity.

No matter what your sins or problems may be, come to Jesus with them. You will look in vain in the gospels for one single case of a sinner who came to Jesus and was rejected. We may be assured on the basis of His Word that this Lord of glory will not cast us aside if we come to Him.

Let us go further to consider this glorious promise of Christ to those who come, "I will in no wise cast out." If Jesus will not cast out a soul that comes to Him, the implication is, of course, that He will receive it. Coming to Christ, we become His and He becomes ours.

What a tremendous encouragement this promise of Christ is to the weary and heavy laden of earth. Living in this world of today so full of distress, unrest, anxiety and fear, what a privilege it is to be a messenger of the Good News! What a joy to give voice to this wonderful proclamation of Christ, "Come unto me all ye that labor and are heavy laden and I will give you rest."

Thousands of souls have answered this call of Christ and out of their experience of His faithfulness they can say:

> I heard the voice of Jesus say,
> "Come unto Me and rest;
> Lay down, thou weary one, lay down
> Thy head upon My breast."
> I came to Jesus as I was,
> Weary and worn and sad;
> I found in Him a resting place,
> And He has made me glad.
>
> H. BONAR

"The master is here and calleth for thee." What is your response to His invitation? To all people of all ages, of all races, Jesus says, "He that comes to me, I will in no wise cast out." He receives all who come to Him that He may save them and keep them all through life and in the vast beyond forever.

One pastor tells of a mother he knew whose son suffered paralysis of the brain; yet, how she loved and cared for him. But the cause of her great grief was this, she said, "I have nursed him from childhood, cleansed, fed and clothed him, watched over him and supplied his every want, tried to please him and to teach him little things and now, though in years he is a man, he does not even know me. He shows no return of my love, but just lies there to eat and drink and sleep! I feel that I cannot go on; I am just looking for some recognition—some response to my lifelong love and care!" How many folks, though not afflicted as that boy, treat their Lord in the same way. They ignore Him and live as though there were no God. They are unmindful of His love and sacrifice, unmindful that every breath they draw is by the grace of God, forgetting that their food, clothing, home, health are all daily gifts from God. Many receive these gifts from God with no recognition of His goodness and with not the slightest response to His love.

But even to those who have neglected the invitation of Christ, to those who have walked the road of unbelief, Jesus says that when they finally do come He will receive them.

If you come to Christ with a heart burdened with a spiritual need, Jesus says emphatically, "I will not cast you out." If you come with a great desire in your heart and take Christ at His word, you will not be repelled.

Bunyan once said, "Oh, the comfort that I have had from this word, 'in no wise,' as who should say, by no means, for no thing, whatever he has done. But Satan would greatly labor to pull this promise from me, telling me that Christ did not mean me. But I should answer him again—Satan, here is, in this Word, no such exception, but him that comes. Him, any him—him that cometh to me I will in no wise cast out!" Bunyan, of course, was right. Christ receives all who come to Him.

Yes, it includes the man down there in skid-row, it includes that one who has been carrying on clandestine affairs. No matter how black your sin, if you come to Christ, He will not cast you out. This truly is the Charter of Christianity, the good news that no case is hopeless, that there is no sinner too bad for Jesus to save.

While visiting a world-famous clinic not long ago, I was impressed by the fact that people were there by the hundreds from all over the world. They came with many strange and to us, at least, unheard-of maladies. In many cases they had come to this clinic as a last resort, having been given up by their local doctors. As one watched them emerge from the consulting rooms, one saw some faces reflecting optimism and hopefulness. They probably had received the word "we can help you." Others came with a look of despair upon their faces. They had heard the sentence that nothing known to medical science could save them. That is the lot of every doctor, to give out life and death sentences. Such is the lot of every physician but one—Jesus the Great Physician. He has never lost a case. He has all power in heaven and earth. It is He alone who "forgiveth all thine iniquities, who healeth all thy diseases, who redeemeth thy life from destruction, who crowneth thee with loving kindness and tender mercies, who satisfieth thy desire with good things so that thy youth is renewed like the eagle" (Ps. 103:3-5).

This glorious Savior, with arms stretched out in love to all mankind, invites you to come to Him that He may save you and keep you now and forever. "He that comes to me, I will in no wise cast out."   AMEN

TWENTY-FOURTH SUNDAY AFTER TRINITY

Then came to him certain of the Sadducees, which deny that there is any resurrection: and they asked him, Saying, Master, Moses wrote unto us, If any man's brother die, having a wife, and he die without children, that his brother should take his wife, and raise up seed unto his brother. There were therefore seven brethren: and the first took a wife, and died without children. And the second took her to wife, and he died childless. And the third took her; and in like manner the seven also: and they left no children, and died. Last of all the woman died also. Therefore in the resurrection whose wife of them is she? for seven had her to wife. And Jesus answering said unto them, The children of this world marry, and are given in marriage: But they which shall be accounted worthy to obtain that world, and the resurrection from the dead, neither marry, nor are given in marriage: Neither can they die any more: for they are equal unto the angels; and are the children of God, being the children of the resurrection. Now that the dead are raised, even Moses shewed at the bush, when he calleth the Lord the God of Abraham, and the God of Isaac, and the God of Jacob. For he is not a God of the dead, but of the living: for all live unto him.

Then certain of the scribes answering said, Master, thou hast well said. And after that they durst not ask him any question at all.

LUKE 20:27-40

Chapter Twenty-one

Shall the Dead Arise?

DURING the public ministry of the Master, He frequently came into contact with the religious leaders of the day. These religious leaders feared that they would lose their hold on the people, and therefore attempted in various ways to discount the teachings of Jesus.

Although there were divisions among these leaders, they interpreted the teachings of the Old Testament to suit themselves. At times they joined hands in order to crush the influence that Jesus had with His followers. At other times one side would join with the Master in order to discount and discredit the views of the other group. Such was the case in the text for our consideration on this Sunday.

The Sadducees, who did not believe in the resurrection of the dead, came to Jesus with a far-fetched question, seeking to entangle Him in His teaching and to gain a point in their favor. Present at this occasion were the chief priests and the scribes. Certain of the scribes belonged to the party known as the Pharisees. The Pharisees were firm believers in the resurrection of the dead. They were happy when Jesus silenced the Sadducees, and they praised Him by saying, "Teacher, thou hast well said."

No doubt Jesus was deeply wounded by this show of division between these leaders of the church, yet He did not refuse to speak with them. Jesus was interested in speaking the truth to them, and He used every opportunity to bring His message to them in order to convince and convict the heart and conscience of His hearers. Jesus speaks to us today, too. He speaks to all men, both sinner and saint, and He would that all men should be saved, and come unto the knowledge of the truth. Let us use every opportunity to bring the message of the pure gospel to mankind; to those who have not heard or will not hear, and to those who have heard but have placed their own interpretations on God's holy Word.

The Sadducees are classified as the rationalists among the Jewish people in Christ's day. They refused to accept and believe in the resurrection of the dead because such a belief was in contradiction to human reason. What they could not reason out, they refused to accept as truth. In order to bring this matter to a head they asked Jesus a complicated question; rather, let us say, they invented the story related in our text. First, they referred to an account found in the twenty-fifth chapter of the book of Deuteronomy, "Master, Moses wrote unto us, If a man's brother die, having a wife, and he die without children, his brother should take his wife, and raise up seed unto his brother." Then they told the invented story of seven brothers, who, one after another, married the same woman in order to fulfill the requirements of the Mosaic law. Then came the question, "Therefore in the resurrection whose wife of them is she? for seven had her to wife."

Now, the Sadducees felt, they had cornered the Master. Certainly He would be unable to get Himself out of this predicament. Jesus answered them, however, by using a line of argument simple and yet profound. The Sadducees did not fully accept all the books of the Old Testament, but they did accept the five books of Moses. Jesus referred them to these books as His authority for teaching the resurrection of the dead. He said, "Now that the dead are raised, even Moses shewed at the bush, when he calleth the Lord the God of Abraham, and the God of Isaac, and the God of Jacob." It must be true then that these men of God still live, "For he is not a God of the dead, but of the living: for all live unto him." There is only one conclusion that may be reached from these words, that there is a life hereafter.

Jesus here gives His sanction to the books of the Old Testament, especially the books of Moses which He refers to in our text. He often referred to the Mosaic law. Then, Jesus firmly let the Sadducees know that in spite of what they taught, He, the Son of God, believed in the resurrection of the dead. He gave them a brief picture of what was in the other world. Thus He silenced them and their objections, giving them the simple and plain truths of His teaching.

We can learn another lesson from the words of our text. After their conversation with Jesus, the Sadducees did not change their views in order to conform to the law of Moses. They continued in their own interpretations, their own belief. How like many people today! They believe what they want to believe, they accept what they want to accept, they reject that which convicts them of their sins. As in the days of our text, we find today many people who must be able to see, touch, and feel everything they accept as being true. Even the divine authority of the Word of God fails to convince them. Think of the millions of misled souls in the world today; those who refuse to accept the entire Word of God, just taking out of God's Word that which is convenient for them to accept and believe. When this fact is pointed out to them, they, like the Sadducees, refuse to change their preconceived ideas, nor will they sacrifice worldly joys and pleasures which they prize so highly, even if these things fall under the judgment of God's holy Word.

Shall the dead arise? Is there a resurrection of the dead? Is there a life hereafter? These and many similar questions have been denied in ages past, even as they are denied in some quarters today. Many do not want to think of a life after death. They want to live for this life alone, so they reject the scriptural fact of the resurrection of the dead.

Job raised the question, "If a man die, shall he live again?" In the Third Article of our Apostles' Creed, the Christian gives his answer to Job's question when he confesses, "I believe in the resurrection of the body."

The word "resurrection" means an awakening or a rising again. In this statement of our Creed, we confess our belief that after our bodies have been laid in the grave and have returned to dust and ashes, they shall be raised up and shall live again, reunited with the souls from which they have been parted. It is God's plan that His children shall in eternity enjoy heaven in their bodies.

Of course, our present bodies, sin-infected, sin-filled and sin-marked as they are, are not fit to be the eternal tabernacle of the soul. They must be changed; they must be purified; they must be glorified. This necessary change takes place in the resurrection. When our bodies are raised from the grave on the great day of resurrection, our bodies will be cleansed from every taint of sin and every effect of sin. Old things will have passed away and all will have become gloriously new.

This is what Paul means when he writes in I Cor. 15:42-44, "So also is the resurrection of the dead. It is sown in corruption; it is raised in incorruption; it is sown in dishonor; it is raised in glory; it is sown in weakness; it is raised in power; it is sown a natural body; it is raised a spiritual body."

The Scriptures teach that in this resurrection change we shall be made like our glorified Savior. "For our conversation is in heaven; from whence also we look for the Savior, the Lord Jesus Christ; who shall change our vile body, that it may be fashioned like unto his glorious body" (Phil. 3:20-21). "We know that, when he shall appear, we shall be like him" (I John 3:2).

The Sadducees could not, and would not, believe this teaching of Jesus. To us the doctrine of the resurrection is not a vague theory, but a clearly revealed truth. Every child of God should hold fast to it with a strong faith. It takes away our dread of the grave and makes us realize that our Christian dead are but "asleep in Jesus."

What about the ungodly, the unbelievers? What about their resurrection? God's Word reveals to us the fact that the ungodly shall also be raised. We must all die, and we must all be raised from our graves. In this respect there is no difference

between the godly and the ungodly. Their graves
from outward appearances may be the same, but
their resurrection will be quite different. The
wicked shall arise unto shame and everlasting contempt. Theirs shall be a resurrection of damnation. Jesus tells us in solemn words, as recorded in
John 5:28-29, "The hour is coming, in the which
all that are in the graves shall hear his voice, and
shall come forth; they that have done good, unto
the resurrection of life; and they that have done
evil, unto the resurrection of damnation."

Let us bear in mind, my friends, that there are
two different paths on which man may travel here
on this earth. These two paths lead to different
resurrections beyond the grave. These resurrections, in turn, are to be followed by two different
states of existence throughout eternity. The one
is the eternal life of the blessed; the other is the
eternal death of the lost.

God's holy Word assures us that He will grant
eternal life to us and to all who believe in Christ.
That person who does not believe this simply does
not believe the gospel. Jesus says, "Verily, verily,
I say unto you, He that believeth on me hath everlasting life" (John 6:47). "As Moses lifted up the
serpent in the wilderness, even so must the Son
of man be lifted up: that whosoever believeth in
him should not perish, but have eternal life"
(John 3:14-15). "My sheep hear my voice, and I
know them, and they follow me: And I give them

eternal life; and they shall never perish, neither shall any man pluck them out of my hand."

Many questions are continually being asked about heaven. Heaven is the name given in Scripture to that home on high which is the abiding place of all those to whom eternal life is given. Our Lord revealed to us the fact that it is a place of unending bliss. These minds of ours cannot even grasp the full meaning of what a glorious place heaven will be. It is a place where there shall be no disappointments nor heartaches. As there is no sin there, there shall be no sickness nor infirmity of any character. No one will use crutches, no one will need glasses in heaven. "God shall wipe away all tears from their eyes; and there shall be no more death, neither sorrow, nor crying, neither shall there be any more pain: for the former things are passed away" (Rev. 21:4).

Heaven means more than merely the absence of the things which cause distress, however; it means also the presence of all those positive blessings these hearts of ours can desire. The Psalmist exclaims, "I shall be satisfied, when I awake, with thy likeness" (Ps. 17:15). We also read in the book of Psalms, "In thy presence is fullness of joy; at thy right hand there are pleasures for evermore" (Ps. 16:11). Perfect happiness, unending happiness with God and His angels and the saints made perfect, that is eternal life in heaven.

What about eternal death? There are many

today who scoff at the idea of eternal punishment, but Scripture tells us that the eternal death of the lost is as plainly taught as is the eternal life of the blessed. Some of the very verses which speak of the bliss of the saved speak also of the misery of the unsaved. "Many of them that sleep in the dust of the earth shall awake, some to everlasting life, and some to shame and everlasting contempt" (Dan. 12:2). "And these shall go away into everlasting punishment: but the righteous into life eternal" (Matt. 25:46). The condition of the ungodly in the future world is called eternal death because it means everlasting separation from God who is the source of life. It means unending remorse and despair. It means misery and torment for body and soul beyond the power of human speech to describe. It is plainly recorded that the loving Jesus shall say to the godless, "Depart from me, ye cursed, into everlasting fire, prepared for the devil and his angels" (Matt. 25:41).

There are those people who ask, "How can the God of love punish sinners eternally?" We must remember that our Lord and Savior would rather pardon than punish. He does everything possible to bring sinners to repentance and to pardon. Being holy, however, He cannot condone sin. He cannot take sin into heaven. Therefore, he who clings to his sins forces eternal death upon himself. The sinner who refuses to accept the pardon, chooses hell.

When the thoughtful Christian confesses that he believes in the life everlasting, he does it with devout thankfulness, not only because he looks forward to the glories of heaven, which he may attain through faith in Jesus Christ as his Savior and Redeemer, but also because he considers the hell which, by the grace of God, he has escaped. The promises of our Savior justifies this faith, for He said, "In my Father's house are many mansions; if it were not so, I would have told you. I go to prepare a place for you. And if I go and prepare a place for you, I will come again, and receive you unto myself; that where I am, there ye may be also. And whither I go ye know, and the way ye know. Thomas saith unto him, Lord, we know not whither thou goest; and how can we know the way? Jesus saith unto him, I am the way, the truth, and the life: no man cometh unto the Father, but by me" (John 14:2-6).

Shall the dead arise? Yes, God has assured us that the dead shall arise. This being true, should we not heed the admonition in Romans 12:1, "I beseech you therefore, brethren, by the mercies of God, that ye present your bodies a living sacrifice, holy, acceptable unto God, which is your reasonable service." God has placed us on this earth, and has given us our bodies for the propagation of the race. We must safeguard them with jealous care. Ennoble your body by observing the laws of health and the laws of morality. Cherish your body as a gift of God that will shower blessings upon you in life, and for the safeguarding of which you will be held eternally responsible. By so doing you will attain to a full and perfect joy in your belief in the resurrection of the body.

Why is it that Christians do not rejoice as they should in the hope of eternal life? Is it because they often fail to honor their bodies as a seed destined to spring up into eternal life? "Whatsoever a man soweth, that shall he also reap." If you are guilty of transgressing the law of God, come to Jesus with your burdens and cares; He will abundantly pardon, He is ever ready to forgive and make you whole. What we give of ourselves to Jesus He will restore to us in a glorified state. What we withhold of ourselves from Him will be lost to us throughout eternity. Let us then give our bodies to Jesus, that He may restore them to us, made like unto His own glorified body. We will be able to do this if we open our hearts to the Spirit of God. Paul says in Romans 8:11, "But if the Spirit of him that raised up Jesus from the dead dwell in you, he that raised up Christ from the dead shall also quicken your mortal bodies by his Spirit that dwelleth in you."

May the Holy Spirit work in our hearts so that our corruptible bodies may be transformed into glorified, eternal bodies like unto the glorified body of Christ our Savior. May we share in the glory of the world to come. AMEN

TWENTY-FIFTH SUNDAY AFTER TRINITY

When ye therefore shall see the abomination of desolation, spoken of by Daniel the prophet, stand in the holy place (whoso readeth, let him understand:) Then let them which be in Judæa flee into the mountains: Let him which is on the housetop not come down to take any thing out of his house: Neither let him which is in the field return back to take his clothes. And woe unto them that are with child, and to them that give suck in those days! But pray ye that your flight be not in the winter, neither on the sabbath day: For then shall be great tribulation, such as was not since the beginning of the world to this time, no, nor ever shall be. And except those days should be shortened, there should no flesh be saved: but for the elect's sake those days shall be shortened. Then if any man shall say unto you, Lo, here is Christ, or there; believe it not. For there shall arise false Christs, and false prophets, and shall shew great signs and wonders; insomuch that, if it were possible, they shall deceive the very elect. Behold, I have told you before. Wherefore if they shall say unto you, Behold, he is in the desert; go not forth: behold, he is in the secret chambers; believe it not. For as the lightning cometh out of the east, and shineth even unto the west; so shall also the coming of the Son of man be. For wheresoever the carcase is, there will the eagles be gathered together.

MATTHEW 24:15-28

Chapter Twenty-two

Jesus Is Coming— Let Us Be Ready

THE coming of Christ, His second Advent, is a part of the blessed hope and the precious faith of the Christian: "He ascended into heaven, and sitteth on the right hand of God the Father almighty: from thence he shall come to judge the quick and the dead."

His second coming is referred to many times in the New Testament, throughout, in almost every book. One book, *Revelation,* is given wholly to this coming of our Savior. It is spoken of with glad expectation: "looking for that blessed hope, and the glorious appearing of the great God and our Savior Jesus Christ." It is cherished for what it will be to the believer: "We shall be like him, for we shall see him as he is; a crown of righteousness is laid up for all that love his appearing." In connection with the description of the second

coming, there is a definiteness of separate events.
Something about the order of their appearance,
and the use of much figurative language has given
occasion for numberless studies, books, and pamphlets, which in large part have led to confusion,
disturbed many, and also caused offense. That is
not strange, perhaps. Think of how misunderstood
was Christ's first coming. The Old Testament had
given many and repeated prophecies of His coming, yet His people were offended by His humble
appearance. The Pharisees looked for worldly
power and glory. Even His best disciples were
slow to understand that the coming of the Savior
was as much for the Gentile as the Jew.

Setting a time or a day for Christ's coming has
especially seemed to attract even earnest souls and
good Bible students. Yet, Jesus spoke in plainest
words, that no one should think, hardly dare, to
try to figure out the day of His coming. Down
through the years men have kept on doing so. It
was a needless, a futile effort, for Jesus said, in
the very chapter of our text, verse 36, "But of
that day and hour knoweth no man, no, not the
angels of heaven, but my Father only." The disciples had asked Jesus, "When?" as to His coming, and for signs, but He didn't answer that part
of their question.

Men have ever tried to make their calculations
and to set a day. A notable instance was that of
the Montanists, a famed sect of the second cen-

tury. They set even the place as well as the day of His coming. Down through the centuries, one day after another has been set, come, but passed with no appearance, in the years 365, 500, 1000, especially, 1350, and in the nineteenth century, many days. Even the noted Bible student, Bengel, set a day in 1836.

In the Middle Ages, and in part at other times, it was not so much the Scriptures on which such calculations were made, as stirring events and times of great disasters, as floods, earthquakes, pestilences.

It has happened, as with the Adventists, that large groups would dispose of their property and gather at some place to await the coming of the Lord. They experienced only disillusionment and in some cases much suffering.

In our own experience, we remember it was said at the time of the first World War, that our publishing house had sold out all they had of books and pamphlets on the end of the world and the second coming of Christ. It is a part of our Christian faith, and we desire to know the time of so great an event. In the stress, trials, sufferings of this life, the hearts of men have turned to the hope, glorious indeed in its promise, for relief and deliverance when Christ comes.

In His answer to the disciples the Lord gave them signs and conditions of His coming. They are impressive, solemn, awful, and of interest for

our study and meditation. Of much more value
and of far greater importance is it to take heed to
ourselves, to prepare our hearts, to be ready when
He comes.

The second coming of Christ is *a great certainty*. The disciples, as they now were leaving
the temple with Jesus, were much impressed with
the building, its big stones, its mighty columns,
its wealth of ornaments and arrangements. His
disciples came to Him, we are told, to show
Him the buildings of the temple. But our Savior,
sad and depressed in spirit, it may be, just having
had an encounter with His enemies, the Pharisees,
saw other things. In all the wealth and strength
and beauty of the temple, Jesus saw its passing,
its transitoriness. Other realities stood before Him.

Evidently the disciples were impressed by the
response of Jesus. They asked Him some questions which brought from Him the great discourse
telling of the destruction of Jerusalem, and of the
end of the world at His coming. These were awful,
terrible certainties, yes, but rich in solemn truth
and helpful guidance, rich in comfort.

The Christian faith is built on things that are
certain, on facts, on things done, being done, and
on things yet to be done. It is on the reality of the
unseen world that the Christian lives. Not only
the buildings of the temple, but even heaven and
earth shall pass away, Jesus tell us. The certainties
on which our faith rests are His Word and all

the wealth and values we have in a God who rules in Providence, who ever lives as our Redeemer, who abides in the blessed communion of saints.

Christ's second coming to bring to an end this world is such a certainty. It is a great certainty, great in its assured appearance, in the terrors for the unbelieving world, in its inexpressible glories for the Christian. As the believer trusts in the finished work of Christ, His death and resurrection, so His second coming is in this same Word assured us for our comfort and hope. It is a great certainty because it is sure. He will appear so all can see Him. Unmistakable, like the lightning as it lights from east to west, so clearly seen it will be. That is all we know about the "when" of His coming. That is enough for every believing soul. It is to be a truth, a promise, sure and unfailing, something to wait for.

There need be no confusion about the reality, the certainty, of His coming. Voices may come from new groups, small groups, new books. We have Christ's own word. Like a thief, not as we think, it will come as the lightning shineth. To be mindful of Christ's certain coming is most wholesome for the hearts of men. To the worldling it is unwelcome and disturbing; to the unconverted it is a serious admonition to repent and to believe; to every Christian it is most wholesome. It emphasizes our personal relation to Christ. It reminds us forcibly that we must all appear before the judgment seat of Christ; it is an earnest admonition to be ready when the Lord comes.

We all know it means much in our everyday life to have something or somebody coming. How much it means for the children that Christmas is coming! How much it means to the weary laborer when night comes and with it, rest. For the youth and maid, for those beginning life, and for those whose life's sun is setting—if we could look into the hearts we would see they live much on what is coming, or what they think is coming.

There is no part of our Christian faith as expressed in the Apostles' Creed that is not of practical help for the daily life of the believer. No one is ever able to take into his conscious faith the richness and fullness of the Christian faith. "Increase our faith," the disciples asked the Lord. Do we not all feel we need to pray in like manner? To some it seems that conversion is all of the Christian life; it is only the beginning. "Grow," says Peter, "in grace and in the knowledge of our Lord and Savior Jesus Christ." In his Second Epistle, he exhorts the believer to add to his faith and virtues. We are many times urged to "increase in wisdom," to be "established" in our faith, so we may "stand in the evil day," or "give an answer" to him who asketh of the hope within us. The second coming of Christ is sure, unmistakable, a coming in power and glory to be seen, a great certainty.

Things about us, a worldly spirit, life that crowds in on us, the struggle to do right and keep clean, cares, fears that weigh on us—all make small or set far away the coming of Christ. It should not be so. It is to be a real, helpful truth, to do for us what many another coming does. It should stir and cheer us, give new courage. It should remind us to set before ourselves the word of the angel, "This Jesus shall come in like manner as ye have seen him go." Surely, when Jesus Himself tells us it is to be like the coming of summer after the cold winter, we realize that most of us have not begun to enter into the glad waiting and comforting hope of the coming of Christ.

But there is a *real danger*. There are dangers, the Lord tells us, dangers at the destruction of Jerusalem, but the same before His coming at the end of the world.

In the year 70 A.D., the Roman General Titus besieged and destroyed Jerusalem. This was prophesied in verse 15 of our text. Something abominable in the eyes of God took place. In the very house of God, a pagan altar was put up and hordes of heathen men desecrated the temple, made it desolate indeed. The Christians were forewarned. They did flee to the little city of Pello across the Jordan, but the multitude of Jews suffered indescribably. The siege was so terrible that fine ladies sought bits of food in garbage heaps. Worse things took place. It was a great tribulation, Jesus says, "such as was not since the beginning of the world to this time, no, nor ever shall be." There will be no time but to flee, without thought of getting a thing with them more than what they had with them. The compassionate heart of Jesus goes out to the mothers with suckling babes or babes unborn. Pray! He exhorts them. Pray that you be spared the flight in winter weather, or on the Sabbath, with its hindrances. God will hear. For, Jesus says, "Except those days should be shortened, there should no flesh be saved," that is, saved for eternity. The Christians, too, would know its terrors, its sufferings, when the end comes.

Many things are spoken of as *signs,* things that will happen. We do not need to know them all, or the order of their coming—good and earnest Christians differ in their view of these things, even able Bible students. The Lord says in speaking of some of these, "Ye shall hear of wars and rumors of wars; see that ye be not troubled." Of other things in a like way; but definitely and repeatedly Jesus warns against something that it seems is seldom mentioned, little noticed, and not greatly feared. He warns against being led astray from the true and saving faith by false teachers.

The first words Jesus speaks in this important discourse are, "Take heed that no man lead you astray. For many shall come in my name, saying, I am the Christ; and shall lead many astray." The

Lord repeats this warning once and again in this long address. These are plain and serious words; *many* shall come, and *many* shall be led astray. That is the danger above all others, for the believer to be led away from Christ.

For our only safety, after all, is to be found in Christ. There is no condemnation to them that are in Christ. So in Luke we read, "Take heed to yourselves, lest haply your hearts be overcharged with surfeiting and drunkenness and cares of this life." There is no other preparation for the coming of Christ than to be a Christian, one to whom Jesus is his refuge, peace, hope.

Christianity is an experience. Luther demonstrated this. There are two cardinal experiences in the Christian life that mark the Christian. How Luther experienced the unrest, the condemnation, the fears of a conscience burdened by sin! That is one experience—sins that trouble so much, to use Jesus' own expression, that we are *sick*, and must go to the Physician, to Jesus. This experience is not the same in degree in everyone, but it is enough when it brings us to Jesus. The other experience, also, Luther knew in large measure. It was the strength, the peace, the joy of his life, his simple trust in Jesus, in His death on the cross for him. When Luther tells about it, he says the good news of Jesus was to him like the open gate of Paradise.

There is no *special* preparation to be made for

the coming of Christ. The Christian is daily prepared for the Lord's coming as he daily seeks
Jesus in prayer, in His Word, and as he in life's
duties and trials and opportunities tries to please
God. That, brother, is to be prepared.

But, take heed, there are many influences that
are strong in leading many astray, and we may
lose Christ now and be lost forever.

There are the cares of life against which Christ
warns us. Note that He places drunkenness and
the cares of life together! Are they to be classed
so? Yes, Jesus does it, although we may feel the
poor man burdened with life's cares is to be ex-
cused. No, the rich man with his many things and
the poor man with little are warned against the
cares of life. They are warned by Jesus who has
enriched many a rich man with better riches than
money can buy, and many a poor man with the
peace and contentment there is in Jesus.

Then there is the wickedness of the world, its
sin and many kinds of evil. These lead men astray.
The Scriptures tell us, in Second Timothy, "In
the last days perilous times shall come. For men
shall be lovers of self, lovers of money, disobedient
to parents, unthankful, without natural affection,
lovers of pleasure more than lovers of God, having a form of godliness, but denying the power
thereof."

As we look at our times and feel the moral
atmosphere of the day, how much of these things

do we see? All our vaunted material abilities and scientific advances—what has it brought the world as we look at the state of things today? There is a marked moral looseness and indifference, which meets us often in carelessness and inefficiency in simple daily duties, more often in the wickedness and crimes of our times. We hear of unnatural crimes, inhuman, sometimes called devilish. We read of mothers killing their children, youths killing their parents, low sex crimes, an increase of drunkenness, a worldly spirit colder and more unfeeling than in many a coarse sinner.

But it is especially the danger that comes from *false teachers* against which we are warned. But how little do we hear about this thing that is to be feared! Yet Jesus admonishes most earnestly against this danger. What is the danger? "Lest you be led astray," says Jesus. So to His own best disciples He speaks and through them to every Christian today.

These false Christs and false prophets speak of religious things. They quote Scripture, sell or give tracts and books. Earnest souls are easily impressed when approached in this way. A man asked the president of a Bible school, "How is it earnest Christians can become Christian Scientists?" He answered, "There are many earnest Christians who are not scripturally intelligent." So they are the easier influenced by one who can talk fast and use much of the Bible in his talk.

Our Savior, when Satan tried to lead Him astray, and even quoted Scripture, was scripturally intelligent. Jesus overcame, as He wants us to overcome, by the use of the sword of the Spirit, the Word of God.

It does make a difference what we believe. What do you believe about Christ? These false teachers seem to realize that they must present a Christ. So they tell their hearers where their "Christ" may be found, often using signs and wonders to prove what they say. But Scripture calls them *lying wonders*. There are unmistakable tests of such false teachers: What do they say of sin, of its presence in all of our thought and life? What do they say of Christ, who by His death on the cross made satisfaction for our sins? Do they make plain that every penitent soul who in an honest confession comes to Jesus will receive the gracious forgiveness of all his sins?

It is true, everlastingly true, that this Christ and Christ alone, can quiet, steady, comfort the heart when that great day comes, be it Christ's return to judge the quick and the dead, or the day of our own death. Only so can we sing,

> Jesus, Thy blood and righteousness
> My beauty are, my glorious dress;
> Midst flaming worlds, in these arrayed,
> With joy shall I lift up my head.
>
> N. L. VON ZINZENDORF

The coming of Jesus is a great and awful certainty. There are, and will be, warnings in the appearing, too often ignored, or not at all noticed. But the coming of Jesus is a definite part of our Christian faith. It is rich in its certain blessings. It is a source of much comfort to the Christian in life's trials and sorrows. It is a wholesome monitor to keep us mindful of the spiritual realities, of things that are not seen, but are eternal. As we look through the New Testament, we learn how real and precious the truth of the second coming was to the saints of old.

It gives the believer something to "look for." We sometimes hear it said of a person, indicating a miserable and pitiable condition, "Poor man! He has nothing to look forward to." But the Christian has something to look forward to. In writing to the Thessalonians, Paul says they have turned unto God from idols, to serve a living and true God, "and to wait for his Son from heaven." To the Corinthians, commending them in much, he says, "Ye come behind in no gift; waiting for our Lord Jesus Christ."

We remember how at the first coming of our Lord at Christmas, we are told by Luke of two old saints of God. Both were among those who were *looking for* something at that coming of the Lord. Simeon was "looking for the consolation of Israel." Anna "spake of him to all that were looking for the redemption of Jerusalem." Paul says in his letter to Titus, the believers are "looking for the blessed hope and appearing of the glory of the great God and our Savior Jesus Christ."

There are those who mock, as Peter says, those who see no signs, and ask, "Where is the promise of his coming?" To them Peter says that God, too, is looking, looking for men to think seriously of themselves before God, looking for men to repent. He gives them time. That is why He waits. We used often to speak of time as a time of grace, time given men to get ready by a true repentance, a turning from sin, a seeking unto Jesus. Shakespeare, too, speaks of such a time of grace.

For we all must stand before the judgment seat of Christ. Each one of us shall give account of himself before God. It is a solemn time, awful for those who know not the Lord, with its fears for every heart.

> Day of wrath! that day of mourning!
> See fulfilled the prophet's warning,
> Heaven and earth in ashes burning!
>
> O what fear man's bosom rendeth,
> When from heaven the Judge descendeth,
> On whose sentence all dependeth.
>
> THOMAS OF SELANO

But, as John tells us, "When he shall appear, we shall be like him"—which we so much have desired to be. We shall be like Him, for we shall see Him as He is. We shall, when He appeareth, receive the crown of glory that fadeth not away. Yes, our bodies, so often slow, lethargic, cumbered with pains and other discomfort, shall be conformed to His glorious body. We, says Peter, "look for new heavens and a new earth." What a contrast that will be to this earth with its injustice and hardness, sickness and the shadows of death, deceit and cruelty. There will be "a new earth, wherein dwelleth righteousness."

Well may James say, "Be patient therefore, brethren, until the coming of the Lord; be patient, establish your hearts, for the coming of the Lord is at hand."

When the Lord comes in His glory, and all the angels with Him, when He is seated on the throne of His glory, with all the nations before Him, He will commend, bless those on His right hand. What for? For things they didn't think much about but did want to do, and *did* do: feed the hungry, visit the sick, take the stranger in, visit those in prison. Surely if these things are coming up on Judgment Day, they are worth while today.

What a joy that will be, how startling to some, as Paul tells us in First Thessalonians, that when the Lord comes He will bring with Him those that have fallen asleep in Jesus.

So at our every celebration of the Sacrament do we proclaim the death of Him who died for us, Him over whom death no more has dominion —we proclaim His death till He comes.

TWENTY-FIFTH SUNDAY AFTER TRINITY

Then shall the kingdom of heaven be likened unto ten virgins, which took their lamps, and went forth to meet the bridegroom. And five of them were wise, and five were foolish. They that were foolish took their lamps, and took no oil with them: But the wise took oil in their vessels with their lamps. While the bridegroom tarried, they all slumbered and slept. And at midnight there was a cry made, Behold, the bridegroom cometh; go ye out to meet him. Then all those virgins arose, and trimmed their lamps. And the foolish said unto the wise, Give us of your oil; for our lamps are gone out. But the wise answered, saying, Not so; lest there be not enough for us and you: but go ye rather to them that sell, and buy for yourselves. And while they went to buy, the bridegroom came; and they that were ready went in with him to the marriage: and the door was shut. Afterward came also the other virgins, saying, Lord, Lord, open to us. But he answered and said, Verily I say unto you, I know you not. Watch therefore, for ye know neither the day nor the hour wherein the Son of man cometh.

MATTHEW 25:1-13

even here there are whole areas of life still un-redeemed.

We need, each of us, years and years of exposure to the power of the Word and Sacraments if, one by one, these unredeemed regions of our lives are to be brought into the focus of consecration to our Lord. Many are turning contentedly to the cross for grace and strength each day, without ever really facing the issue of our Lord's sacrifice in relation to their social life, their bank accounts, the race question, or their home problems. At some such point all of us have either overlooked, or we have been unwilling to see, Christ's redemption applied where we are failing.

One may quote statistics to any purpose. There are many to show that what has been done by the Church since she was given her marching orders by her Lord is an imposing record. When we measure what is still left undone of His commission, however, it is clear that we have been unprofitable servants. Perhaps the impact of these unfinished tasks, as they were brought home to us each Sunday of the Trinity season, has only lulled us into a stupor of despair. There is much to do; there are few to do it. Is there any use in making the effort? If we are asking that question, we must have forgotten that with the command to conquer for Him, Jesus also promised, "Lo, I am with you alway, even to the end of the world."

In these last Sundays of the church year, the

gospels have brought us, by almost imperceptible degrees, face to face with the truth confronting us in the parable of the ten virgins. Despite the fact that the Church is a long way from fulfillment of its tasks, the truth is that our day of grace may end at any moment. Despite the leisurely pace we have taken in the work of the Church, there is an urgency about its fulfillment that bids us not to tarry. "Watch therefore, for ye know not the day nor the hour." There is no time to waste. Every moment counts and must be made to count against the assignment to bring every area of every life under the Lordship of Christ.

"The peace that passeth understanding" must not be permitted to become a sheath for the weapon of time. The security under the Shepherd's staff must not make us love the green pastures so much that we avoid the rocky descent into the valley. Patience and contentment must be distinguished from complacency and heedlessness. The sense of gratitude for the blessings of this life must not deaden our expectation of the incomparably greater blessings of eternity.

At this point occurs the greatest hazard for all men, even for those in the Church. Days and months and years have a way of sliding by us silently, like a gentle stream, assuring us that they will always continue to do the same. "There are many more where we come from," they whisper to us as they pass. We take their lie into our bosoms, closing our ears to the sounds of destruction all around us as, one by one, our friends and relatives answer the call to judgment.

The tragedy is that man can settle down so cozily to enjoy the earth when heaven is his destination. Consider the foolishness of our ancestors if, setting sail for America, they had adjusted themselves so thoroughly to the hardships of the voyage that they neglected to prepare for disembarking. What if they had chosen to stay aboard, neither returning to the home from which they had set out so purposively, nor arriving at their destination, but contenting themselves only with the journey? Scripture often refers to life as a journey and most often as a "walk" in which every step brings us closer to the end. We can never retrace our steps in this walk. "We pass this way but once." Waking or sleeping, we plod on without stopping to rest, however intriguing the scenery and associations along the way may be. At last we reach the end of that walk, and we stand before our God.

Yet, we like to imagine that we have settled down permanently even before we have fairly begun our journey. To bolster this self-deceit we build snug homes and establish places of business. We acquire an address and settle down at our fireside in the evening, confident that however fiercely the storm of time may howl out there in the night, we are safe and secure against it within our cozy home. But even there we are plunging steadily onward to our destination. The ticking of the clock on the mantel matches the beating of our hearts. Both of them will finally complete their given task and stop. This earth is not our destination. We are bound for an eternal kingdom for which every moment must make us ready.

In Christ's Church this has always been a joyous certainty which has sometimes burned brightly, sometimes weakly, but has never died out entirely. In the early Apostolic Church the hope of the Lord's imminent second coming was the basis of the very greeting with which the Christians encouraged one another. "Maranatha," they said, "The Lord cometh!" They lived a hazardous life because of their faith, and that faith made martyrs of many of them. In the midst of such hostile surroundings, the end of their world and the coming of Christ were happy thoughts. Expecting every day to meet their Lord, and suffering great hardship because of their trust in Him, their faith dared magnificently the promises He had given them. His words, "Whosoever loseth his life for my sake shall find it," were not merely a philosophical proposition to them. They were a certainty to which they committed themselves in daring practice. Certain that Christ would redeem every promise, the only thing they could not risk was disbelief. That would have taken away the only thing which gave their suffering meaning. That would destroy their only hope that there would be an end to the ceaseless struggle against their own perversity. So they clung to the certainty that, although the Bridegroom tarried, He would come at any moment and would find them ready to meet Him. Though it might cost them their lives, they dared not be unprepared for His coming day or night.

Even in those heroic days of the Church, however, there were "foolish virgins"—those to whom the crisis of such a dangerous faith was superfluous and needlessly spectacular. It was nobody else's business what *they* believed. They would keep their faith in Christ who had given and promised them so much, but they would keep it to themselves and not confide it wherever they went, as if they were looking for trouble. As for Christ's second coming, He had delayed so long already that it was quite likely that He would tarry longer. Meanwhile, there were comforts and pleasures to be found even in this life. Why should they not enjoy them as much as possible?

The only trouble was that in hiding their faith they lost it. In looking for the comforts and pleasures in this life they lost sight of the hope of eternal life. It was the age-old risk that they ran, of substituting the journey for the destination, of throwing away the end because of the means.

The patriarchs of the Old Testament had almost lost their way in this falsehood of Satan. As

long as time remains that wicked one will seduce
men with his impossible promises of a crown without a cross, and of the all-sufficiency of time. "Re-
nunciation is too childish for intelligent adults,"
he whispers to those who have well-begun their
journey in life. "Leave that grandstand-play to
the young people. There will always be ample
time to give up the non-essentials. You must be
realistic about this for you live in a real world,
not an unreal."

To youth he whispers unctuously, "Now let's
not get too serious-minded all at once. There's
time enough for that when you are middle-aged
and have a family of your own. You are young
only once, and no one wants to cheat you out of
the full enjoyment of these wonderful years of
your life. There will be plenty of time for being
serious later on."

To old age his whisper is just as deceptive,
"Now don't get panicky. Everything depends
upon keeping calm. You are to avoid excitement
at your time of life. After all, you have lived a
good life and raised a fine family. What have you
to worry about? You have worked all your life;
now relax and enjoy the things you have worked
for so hard. One of these days, of course, you will
get sick and eventually you will die. But there
will be plenty of time then to settle things with
God."

All of us who are in the Church have had a

glimpse of the truth about the importance of our destination, and we do want to keep open some lines of communication to the eternity that has such glorious hopes. There are many of us, however, who are like the foolish virgins in Jesus' parable. They wanted to be in the party when the bridegroom came, but they were sure that they could arrange to get oil for their lamps when that time arrived.

But salvation cannot be improvised. It was forged, and Calvary was the anvil, my sins were the sledge hammer. The arm of a just God delivered the blows that forged it. However, the wrath of God fell not upon me, but upon the Substitute who stepped into my place and bore the blows which belonged to me. The anguish of my Substitute and yours was matched only by His cry of triumph when His mission was complete. "It is finished" is the first sentence of the last chapter in the Book of Redemption which began to be written when Adam and Eve had sinned. Salvation was not improvised; it was worked out step by anguishing step in the heart of a loving God until it was finally performed excruciatingly in the sacrifice of Jesus Christ. It was then completed, and the Resurrection was the final and irrevocable proof of its completion. Who am I, who are you, to imagine that we can contrive that which cost the very life-blood of God?

Much less can we borrow this salvation from

others. "Christianity is always one generation away from extinction," because it is not an inheritable life. The heritage we give to our children is that of our nature, a perverse and rebellious opposition to God's will. Jesus said, "Except a man be born again he cannot see the kingdom of God." God has no grandchildren, but He is ready to make all of us His own children through His only begotten Son. That means that the miracle of a new birth must be performed in each of us so that the recalcitrance of the natural heart may be met by the eager obedience of the new life in Christ. His Spirit lives in hearts, not hearths; His faith is for individuals, not families or nations or peoples.

"Give us of your oil; for our lamps are going out." Jesus identifies this petition with the foolish virgins for it is not in the power of men to grant it. Only from God can the miracle of a new birth proceed. Many a parent would give his very life if he could impart his faith to a wayward child. Many a pastor has agonized at a bedside to minister to a dying man that which only God can bestow. How desperate such moments are! But the prayer of a soul which has delayed so long must find its way to the throne where the Savior of sinners is seated at the right hand of the Father. If we will not turn to Him for the salvation we need, then wherever else we turn our most anguishing prayers will come back to us empty.

The world waited thousands of years for the Savior to be born, and most of the world did not even know for whom it waited. But in the fullness of time He came with the answer to every prayer and a mission for every life. Thank God, He did not tarry then until our day. Coming as a Savior He proclaimed liberty for our slavery and atonement for our sins.

But that mission is complete! When He comes again He will come as a Judge. For all who have not met Him as Redeemer, it will be a fearful thing to stand before Him and to hear Him say, "Verily, I say unto you, I know you not." How can He know us if we have never come to Him? He came, knocking at our door, to offer us salvation but we would not open to Him. How urgently we need His redemption now, before the watchman announces that He has come! Heaven is our intended destination. Will we choose any other?

"Watch therefore, for ye know not the day nor the hour." Jesus closes His parable with these words with which the faithful in all ages since have been warned against complacency. It is our "alert" when every instinct speaks of security. "Blessed is that servant, whom his lord when he cometh shall find so doing."

We make a terrible mistake, however, if we understand this "watching" to consist in an irresponsible and idle waiting on some convenient hill top for Christ's appearance. When Christ had ascended into heaven His disciples stood looking into the sky where they had lost sight of Him. An angel appeared and rebuked them, "Why stand ye gazing up into heaven? This same Jesus shall so come in like manner as ye have seen Him go into heaven." Then they remembered Jesus' parting command to them to be witnesses unto Him in Jerusalem, in Judea, in Samaria, and unto the uttermost parts of the earth as soon as the Holy Spirit had been given to them.

This is what our Lord will find the faithful doing when He comes again. This is the task that stretches out so formidably before His Church. To be witnesses unto Him at home and abroad, in every area of life, that His kingdom may come among all men; this is the task of the Church.

How busy she is! Foreign missionaries are risking their lives to preach the gospel and to bring the ministry of healing to "the least" of the brethren of Christ. Men and women are burning out their lives in Christ's service as teachers on our Christian campuses. Folks are devoting a life of ceaseless activity for His sake to the poor, the aged, the infirm, the orphaned and the widowed—all for the sake of their Savior. Men and women are opening the doors of their hearts and their homes to the oppressed and dispossessed of other lands —because they love their Lord. People are revising their attitudes toward other races and classes. They are changing their amusement habits. They are opening their purses and giving both of their abundance and their need for the kingdom.

They are setting aside in a busy and demanding daily schedule a time for reading their Bibles and for prayer—all in the response of grateful hearts to the gift of a completed salvation. Men, women, and children are gathering together each Lord's Day to listen to His Word, to worship Him, and to receive marching orders for another week. Christian people are discovering the strengthening grace and comfort in the Sacrament by which the understanding Savior, who would not leave us comfortless, provided for His real presence with the believers until He should come again in glory.

No one is so busy doing his uncomplaining best as the Christian in this world of uncompleted assignments. Soon, he knows, the shout will be raised that the Bridegroom comes, and his lamp, refilled through its very use, will be found burning brightly. He is not standing still, gazing up into heaven. He knows that heaven, not this weary and wicked world, is his true destination; and he will not rest until his earthly task is done, whether it be great or small. "Blessed is that servant, whom his lord when he cometh shall find so doing." For then they will go before Him with well-trimmed lights into the glory of eternity, where the unutterable praise of God's glory and His love will be sung before the throne of grace. Nicolai pictures the scene in his hymn:

Hear Thy praise, O Lord, ascending
From tongues of men and angels, blending
  With harp and lute and psaltery.
By Thy pearly gates in wonder
We stand, and swell the voice of thunder,
  In bursts of choral melody:
No vision ever brought,
No ear hath ever caught,
  Such bliss and joy:
We raise the song, we swell the throng,
To praise Thee ages all along.

AMEN

TWENTY-FIFTH SUNDAY AFTER TRINITY

Heaven and earth shall pass away, but my words shall not pass away.

But of that day and hour knoweth no man, no, not the angels of heaven, but my Father only. But as the days of Noe were, so shall also the coming of the Son of man be. For as in the days that were before the flood they were eating and drinking, marrying and giving in marriage, until the day that Noe entered into the ark, And knew not until the flood came, and took them all away; so shall also the coming of the Son of man be. Then shall two be in the field; the one shall be taken, and the other left. Two women shall be grinding at the mill; the one shall be taken and the other left.

Watch therefore: for ye know not what hour your Lord doth come. But know this, that if the goodman of the house had known in what watch the thief would come, he would have watched, and would not have suffered his house to be broken up. Therefore be ye also ready: for in such an hour as ye think not the Son of man cometh.

Matthew 24:35-44

Chapter Twenty-four

He Is Coming Again!

STREET lights sprout evergreens, colored lights are strung across busy avenues, carols echo through the air in almost every city and town weeks before Advent begins. Men, women, and children everywhere are reminded that the happy Christmas season is approaching and it is time to get ready for that great day. Newspapers carry full-page ads; crowded department stores have new glitter and dazzle. No matter who the individual, rich man or poor man, employer or employee, teacher or student, he is caught in the whirl of activity which is supposed to remind us to prepare for the coming of the Christ-child. Would to God that there were as much time and preparation of heart and soul, as much effort put into understanding the *real* significance which the weeks ahead should have for us all!

Jesus told us of another day which is coming. He often spoke about it. It is a day for which there

265

should be much preparation. It is a day for which every man, woman, and child should watch and be ready. For He is coming again. He is coming, not as a child in Bethlehem's manger, but in visible glory, and all the holy angels will be with Him. He shall sit upon the throne of His glory. Everyone will see Him and know Him. There will be no doubt as to who He is, and what He will do.

The important thing is—are we ready for Him? Are we living a life acceptable to Him? Are we living a life so occupied with the things of this world that we pay no attention to, nor care, whether He is coming again or not? Will He be returning to hearts that are cold and unreceptive?

This great text is prophetic, and Jesus warns us to take heed. He tells us unqualifiedly of the certainty of His coming. He declares that the time of His coming is known only to the Father. He repeatedly emphasizes the fact that it will take the world by surprise, and that His own people ought always to be ready to meet Him.

That Jesus is coming again is certain. He Himself said so. "The disciples came unto him privately, saying, Tell us, when shall these things be? and what shall be the sign of thy coming, and of the end of the world?" (v. 3). He told them a number of astounding things that would happen before He comes again. Nation would rise against nation, kingdom against kingdom; there would be famine, pestilence, and earthquakes; false

Christs would arise. In the world in general there would be spiritual indifference, ungodliness, false security, and materialism. These signs have appeared before, many times, but they will appear with intensity and frightful proportions as never before when the end comes.

As if to drive home the truth of His statements, He adds, "Heaven and earth shall pass away, but my words shall not pass away" (v. 35). No book has foretold the course of events or the destiny of peoples long centuries in advance with such accuracy and precision as do the Scriptures. This fact alone should be proof of the divine origin of God's Word which so clearly foresees the future.

The Bible is full of promises. This is one of them. Jesus promises that He is coming again. The value of a promise depends on the integrity of the one who makes the promise and his ability to fulfill it. There is no question regarding God's integrity or ability. The promises contained in His Word are great and precious. They have always been fulfilled in the past. The truth of the Old and New Testaments is final. God has kept His pledges despite His enemies and the anxious perplexities of His children. Prophets of old foresaw the end of godless nations in their day. Isaiah predicted that the proud city of Babylon with its great walls, its beautiful temples, its massive gates and impregnable fortresses would be destroyed. Soon after the prophecy was made, Babylon's magnificent splendor collapsed in terrifying destruction. God keeps His Word. The stories of Nineveh, Jericho, and Jerusalem are but parts of a long record of prophecies fulfilled. God keeps His Word. The gospels give the most striking fulfillment of prophecy and promises when they record the glorious and literal enactment of Jesus' birth, life, death, and resurrection. God keeps His Word. Both the Old and New Testaments abound with predictions of the future that were fulfilled hundreds and thousands of years later with minute and mathematical accuracy.

"Heaven and earth shall pass away, but my words shall not pass away." His words never fail. Therefore the certainty of the fact that He is coming again! Since God's promises have been valid up to now, it follows that they will hold for the future. But, what about the promise that He is coming again? The Church has been waiting for centuries for His coming in glory, not to establish a golden era upon this earth, but to "judge the quick and the dead" (as we confess in our Creed) and to bring the faithful into their heavenly heritage. Just as surely as the light follows the darkness, so the Day of the Lord, sudden and unexpected, will break upon the world.

He is coming again in God's appointed time. "Of that day and hour knoweth no one, not the angels of heaven, neither the Son, but the Father only" (v. 36).

We cannot predict the day or the hour when Christ will come again. Many have tried it and failed. I remember, as a young, impressionable teen-ager, for lack of something better to do one night, I slipped into the back row of a tent meeting conducted by some sect. The topic for the evening was "The Second Coming." Whatever else was said that night is forgotten, but this left an indelible impression—that Jesus was coming the next Saturday night at nine o'clock. With what assurance and earnestness that man spoke! I told some of my close friends. Saturday night we sat on the curbstone waiting for something terrible to happen. As the hour approached we looked into the heavens, expecting Jesus to come. We were frightened. We wondered if we would ever see our folks again. Nothing happened. The hour passed, but the end of the world didn't come. We went home —and that tent meeting moved to another part of the city. Another of many attempts on the part of man to prophesy the time of His coming had come to naught.

No man, nor the angels in heaven, neither the Son, knows the time of His coming again. When Jesus said that not even the Son knows of the day or the hour, we must remember that He had a human as well as a divine nature, and it was according to His human nature, when He voluntarily renounced the full use of His divine attributes, that He spoke these words to His disciples.

No, we cannot tell when Christ will return. "It is not for you to know the time or the seasons, which the Father hath put in his own power."

But some general signs of His coming are given, and they are of a distressing nature. "And as were the days of Noah, so shall be the coming of the Son of Man" (v. 37). It is difficult to know how wicked and vile men had become in Noah's day. The Word of God does not attempt to describe or catalog their sins. We have heard some awful things about the horrors of the Buchenwald prison camp during the last war, and we have shuddered and wondered how beastly man can become. It must have been far worse in Noah's day. In one awful sentence, in which almost every word is a vivid picture of the intensity of evil, Scripture simply states, "And God saw that the wickedness of man was great in the earth, and that every imagination of the thoughts of his heart was only evil continually" (Gen. 6:5). Man had gone the extreme limit of human depravity. The deluge of wickedness and corruption and evil had reached the point where only a deluge of water could wash away from the earth its vileness, so carnal, sensual, and devilish. The patience of a long-suffering God was finally exhausted.

"They were eating and drinking, marrying and giving in marriage, until the day Noah entered into the ark." The period before the second coming of Christ will resemble the time before the flood while the ark was being built. Men will be concerned about worldly affairs. It isn't wrong to eat and drink and marry, but when men live only for these things, then they lose themselves in worldly pursuits and forget the spiritual. Then comes gross materialism, and along with that, moral laxity. With moral corruption come lawlessness and violence. How obvious this has been in all the terrifying violence and cruelty of the past decades. Surely the lawlessness, not only of individuals but of nations as well, is that "spirit" of lawlessness which is a sign of the times. Disobedience, rebellion against God, and perversion of the truth are all outstanding characteristics of the last days.

Jesus' words should cause us to take inventory of our own day. Are we becoming a cynical, sophisticated, self-satisfied people that knows not the God of our fathers? When we honestly look back over the past century, we see how God blessed us with parents who were men and women with vision. They depended upon God. They believed that God led them. They founded our congregations and built most of our churches. They established our Christian schools. They had convictions; were willing to do hard work; were willing to sacrifice. They were praying men and women who built for their day and the future. They knew God and recognized His providential deliverance, the certainty of His judgments, and the boundlessness of His grace.

Does our day bear the marks of Noah's generation? God has been good to us. He has showered His gifts upon us. We have much of everything. We have comfortable homes, the largest cars, the best radios, the most modern conveniences. We push buttons, and machines do our work. We have more comforts, more attractions, more opportunities, more conveniences than any generation before us. We pride ourselves on these things. We work and slave to get the dollars that will buy them. We are driven by the desire to accumulate material things. We worship the idols of mass production and the so-called "almighty dollar." Are we, as a result, a selfish, greedy, sensual generation that will have to face tragic consequences?

With all this, are we forgetting God? Morally we are breaking down. Just read your newspapers for evidence. When fear of God is removed from the hearts of the people, and when a keen sense of sin is gone and God's Word is ignored, then there must be real concern for what lies ahead. He is coming again in God's appointed time.

"Watch therefore . . . be ye also ready." We are certain Christ is coming again in God's own appointed time, when everyone will appear before Him for final judgment. He will come unannounced; it will be an instantaneous, silent moving of God's dynamic power. His coming will be sudden. The people of Noah's day "knew not until the flood came, and took them all away"

peace of heart that comes only in knowing Christ as Savior. Have you thought of speaking to a friend, or relative, who has become indifferent or cold spiritually? The opportunities are legion to be a watchman for the Lord Jesus Christ. The world is full of lonely souls ready to listen to the proclamation of the love of God. There is work to be done. There is a soul for you to see—now. When Jesus returns there will be no time to repent for sin nor make restitution. There will be no time then to win souls and lead them to the cross. There will be no time then to pray. We must work while it is day, for the night cometh!

Are *we* ready to receive Him when He comes again? This is the vital question of our text. It is personal. No one can answer it for us. Membership in a church or any of its organizations does not make us ready. Doing good works, contributing to philanthropic enterprises, trying to live a good life—these do not make us ready for Him. These follow when we take the all-important step of accepting Jesus as our personal Lord and Savior. This text invites us to be ready when He comes. It pleads with those of us who have come from Christian homes but have lost the faith that our God-fearing parents had. It pleads with those of us who have been members of the Church of Jesus Christ, but who have permitted the attractions and cares of this life to crowd out our duties and responsibilities to the God who wants our souls. It pleads with those of us who may feel that we are so far gone in sin that the grace of God cannot reach us. Be ye ready to receive Him! Christ, the friend of sinners, pleads with us to change our ways—turn from our lust for power, for money, for material things, to the inestimable riches which He offers. Come in repentance and faith before it is too late. Christ reaches out to bestow upon us all that our heart ever yearned for—happiness, contentment, His never-failing, never-ending grace, and that peace which passes all understanding.

How can you be ready? Listen to the words of one of the most wonderful promises: "We are justified freely, by his grace, through the redemption which is in Christ Jesus, his Son!" Take into your heart the most wonderful gift ever offered to man. Come trusting, believing in Him. If you have never known what it means to have the blessed assurance of being ready whenever He might come, if you have never felt the happiness and joy of looking for His coming, then the same Lord who urges you to "be ready" calls out to you now, "Come unto me! Follow me!" Obey that call, my friend, and you need not trouble yourself about the time of His coming. Then you will be ready.

AMEN

TWENTY-SIXTH SUNDAY AFTER TRINITY

At that time Jesus answered and said, I thank thee, O Father, Lord of heaven and earth, because thou hast hid these things from the wise and prudent, and hast revealed them unto babes. Even so, Father: for so it seemed good in thy sight. All things are delivered unto me of my Father: and no man knoweth the Son, but the Father; neither knoweth any man the Father, save the Son, and he to whomsoever the Son will reveal him.

Come unto me, all ye that labor and are heavy laden, and I will give you rest. Take my yoke upon you, and learn of me; for I am meek and lowly in heart: and ye shall find rest unto your souls. For my yoke is easy, and my burden is light.

MATTHEW 11:25-30

Chapter Twenty-five

Come Unto Me

THE verses preceding our text reveal that Jesus' invitation had been rejected by many to whom His heart had gone out in love and compassion. The attitude of the people of Chorazin and Bethsaida may be summarized in the awful statement —"they repented not" (Matthew 11:20). The very cities which had been most privileged in hearing His Word and beholding His works of power refused to repent and so continued in their sins. No wonder their judgment will be more severe than that of Tyre and Sidon. What a warning to us! We dare not hear the Word of God in vain— the greater our privilege of knowing the truth, the more terrible the punishment if we reject that truth. Though despised and rejected by so many, Jesus was not "soured." He did not give up because some treated Him coldly and ungratefully. He came to do His Father's will, and He did not turn back. In our words for this day Jesus invites,

"Come unto me." When we come we receive at least three blessings: We are to come for wisdom. Jesus invites, "Come unto me" for revelation of the Father and the Son. Jesus invites, "Come unto me" for rest.

We Are to Come for Wisdom

At the very time Jesus was experiencing the bitterness of men's indifference and opposition, He turns in praise to the Father, rejoicing that though the great ones in Israel rejected Him the humble received His words. His words are, "I thank thee, O Father." How wonderful! The everlasting and loving Son of God praises His Father for the remnant that would receive Him. He knows that everything will be fulfilled and that His death will not be in vain. What a challenge this is to us, that Jesus could praise God even in the midst of rejection. Often we become filled with melancholy when grief, fear, and disappointment beset us. The way out is to praise the Lord. One man of God who was severely tried thanked the Lord for His love and prayed, "Lord Jesus, I thank you that it is no worse than it is."

We are invited, today, to come with all confidence, and know that He is able to do for us far above that which we can ask or think, and that He is able to defend us in every time of need and evil. If we come we, too, shall be able to say, "I thank Thee, O Father." The great and deep, yet simple truths of the gospel are often hid from the worldly wise. "The world by wisdom knew not God" (I Corinthians 1:21). A man may be ever so learned in the mysteries of God, nature, and state, and yet be ignorant of the mysteries of the kingdom of heaven.

In his unsaved condition Paul knew much about God, but he did not know the God and Father of our Lord Jesus Christ. He did not know Him until he became a babe and was willing to let the Holy Spirit reveal unto him his need. Christ chose the foolish things of the world to proclaim the gospel, not the learned men of the world. The reason spiritual truth is hid from the wise and prudent is that they rest in their own wisdom and not in the revealed wisdom of God. If they allow the Holy Spirit to reveal the truth, their understanding is opened and they perceive the truth of God. Jesus was completely resigned to the will of His Father and, therefore, was able completely to carry out the Father's will. It is only as we submit our all and pray, "Even so, Father," that we as babes receive the truth. Thank God that through babes who are willing to be led and receive all truth from God, He reveals His plan for men through the foolishness of preaching. However, God's people must not remain babes; as they feed on the Word and are obedient to His will they grow in grace, wisdom, and usefulness.

Jesus Says, "Come Unto Me" for Revelation of the Father and the Son

God, in His great plan, has so arranged that He can only be understood and received through His Son Jesus. To Jesus, God has given all power in heaven and earth. When we come to God, in the name of Jesus, He receives us and gives us the treasures of His grace. In Jesus we have everything that God has given to His Son. How good it is to know Christ. As one man has said, "The Father has delivered His all into the hands of the Lord Jesus: let us also deliver our all into His hand, and the work is done." He is the fullness of life, the life abundant that God wants to give. It is sad that men do not see this. They desire to save their life in their own way, and to do so is to lose out completely. When we lose our all in Christ and are identified with Him, we live eternally. Outside of Jesus there is no revelation of the Father. He and He alone makes us pleasing in God's sight. Many have lost sight of this great and eternal truth. They speak of a fatherhood of God and a brotherhood of man—but Jesus, the only One who can reveal the Father and make men brothers, is stripped of His divinity, honor and Saviorhood. We should be thankful that we may hear, read, and receive unto ourselves the blessed truth of Christ's revelation of Himself to men.

Jesus Also Invites, "Come Unto Me" For Rest

These truths revealing Christ and His glory are not merely objective. Jesus also invites us to salvation and rest, and is concerned that we personally experience His grace. That is why He says, "Come unto me, all ye that labor and are heavy laden, and I will give you rest." God's Word from cover to cover is one urgent invitation to sinners to come to God for salvation. What joy that this gospel is still being preached. However, only those who labor and are heavy laden will come to Jesus for rest. This is an invitation to all who realize that they are sinners and are crushed by its awful pressure. Those who are sick of their sin, tired of serving the devil and who desire peace and forgiveness are invited to Jesus in the words, "Come unto me."

This is the same invitation extended in Revelation 22:17, "And the Spirit and the bride say, Come. And let him that heareth say, Come. And let him that is athirst come. And whosoever will, let him take the water of life freely." Before we can experience rest, we must know the awfulness of distress. Before we can be healed we must be torn. A certain man lay upon his death bed. He was satisfied that all was well. He had lived a good life and was thankful that he would soon enter the eternal rest. His pastor sought to show him that his good life could not save him, that he was a sinner who needed Jesus. The sick man insisted

that all was well, because he had never done anything wrong. All debts were paid, and his will had
been made. What more could be expected than
this? The pastor prayed that God might reveal
to him a word that should be spoken. Immediately
this thought flashed, and he turned to the sick
man and said, "You might as well stop hoping
for the best; you are a sinner and you will be
eternally lost." This strong statement given by
God was the means used by the Holy Spirit to
open his eyes. He began to realize his awful condition. Soon he became weary and heavy laden.
Then it was easy for that pastor to lead him to
Christ who gave him rest.

Outside of Jesus there is no rest. There may
be a false rest, but true rest is only to be found in
Jesus. Christ is our Noah, whose name signifies
rest. Resting in Jesus we are free from the terror
and power of sin. We are at peace in His love.
This is the rest of Hebrews 4:9, begun here and
perfected in glory. Our prayer should be, "Lord
Jesus, show men that outside of Thee they are
laboring and heavy laden—press this home, Lord,
until they find their rest in Thee." When we have
His rest, we are released from the drudgery of
sin and receive not only a crown for our head, but
also a yoke for our neck. To take Christ's yoke is
to discover that sin's heavy burden is removed and
that subjection to Christ is rest indeed. His yoke
is lined with love, and we find that we are one

with Him who is the Lover of our souls. Many fear Christ's yoke; they think that receiving it will involve them in greater sacrifices than they are able or ready to make. How false this is! Jesus says, "My burden is light." Paul knew much of affliction for Christ's sake. Still, in II Corinthians 4:17, he calls it a "light affliction." In Christ we are never alone and, come what may, He shoulders the burden for us.

One man who had suffered much finally found rest in Jesus. His suffering continued as before, but now he could say, "My burden is light, Jesus suffers for me." He had learned the secret of identification with Christ. In this blessed relationship Jesus teaches us daily the secrets of His Word. He is patient and gentle. He will never rush or push us, but will continually unfold to us the glory and beauty of Himself. While we gaze at Him we ourselves are transformed. We see how heavy laden the unsaved really are, we are consumed with a Holy Spirit desire to serve God, and our prayer becomes, "Lord Jesus, use me when and where and as Thou wilt." As we learn of Him, we begin to realize more fully the purpose of His coming and dying that all might be saved. Then as we are used, we discover that truly to serve Him is rest indeed, and we agree that His yoke is easy and His burden light. What joy and rest to know that we are in His will and that we shall see Him some day.

Let us summarize briefly what this rest is. The rest that Jesus gives is twofold. It is rest of conscience, because the sin question is settled. It is a rest of heart. This is calm in the midst of storm. These two rests are the same as the two aspects of peace presented in the Epistles. Rest of conscience is the equivalent of that peace *with* God which belongs to all who are justified by faith (Romans 5:1). Rest of soul is the same as that peace *of* God which passes all understanding (Philippians 4:6-7). This is enjoyed by all who commit their all to Jesus.

Jesus' invitation is—"Come unto me." It is urgent and loving. May our response be—"Just as I am, I come, I come!"

AMEN

TWENTY-SIXTH SUNDAY AFTER TRINITY

*When the Son of man shall come in his glory, and all
the holy angels with him, then shall he sit upon the
throne of his glory: And before him shall be gathered
all nations: and he shall separate them one from another,
as a shepherd divideth his sheep from the goats: And
he shall set the sheep on his right hand, but the goats
on the left. Then shall the King say unto them on his
right hand, Come, ye blessed of my Father, inherit the
kingdom prepared for you from the foundation of the
world: For I was an hungred, and ye gave me meat: I
was thirsty, and ye gave me drink: I was a stranger, and
ye took me in: Naked, and ye clothed me: I was sick,
and ye visited me: I was in prison, and ye came unto
me. Then shall the righteous answer him, saying, Lord,
when saw we thee an hungred, and fed thee? or thirsty,
and gave thee drink? When saw we thee a stranger, and
took thee in? or naked, and clothed thee? Or when saw
we thee sick, or in prison, and came unto thee? And the
King shall answer and say unto them, Verily I say unto
you, Inasmuch as ye have done it unto one of the least
of these my brethren, ye have done it unto me. Then
shall he say also unto them on the left hand, Depart
from me, ye cursed, into everlasting fire, prepared for the
devil and his angels: For I was an hungred, and ye gave
me no meat: I was thirsty, and ye gave me no drink: I
was a stranger, and ye took me not in: naked, and ye
clothed me not: sick, and in prison, and ye visited me
not. Then shall they also answer him, saying, Lord,
when saw we thee an hungred, or athirst, or a stranger,
or naked, or sick, or in prison, and did not minister unto
thee? Then shall he answer them, saying, Verily I say
unto you, Inasmuch as ye did it not to one of the least
of these, ye did it not to me. And these shall go away
into everlasting punishment: but the righteous into life
eternal.*

MATTHEW 25:31-46

Chapter Twenty-six

Before the Judgment Throne of God

CHRIST confronts us with the realities of life and death, of heaven and hell, and answers many of our questions about His purposes for us in this description of Judgment Day. We see Christ as the great King and Judge, surrounded by the holy angels, and with all the nations of the world before Him to hear His final judgment which will either commit them to eternity in hell or summon them to the eternal joys of heaven. It is as though God permits us to stand on a hill apart from the judgment scene and view the most dramatic event of all history. Of all events past and future only the creation of the world and the passion of Christ compare with the judgment of the nations, and this may be said to be the goal of both. This tremendous event we shall witness with our own eyes, for we shall be there. We see here in retrospect the terrific struggle in the hearts of all men, that of God versus the world, and we see the decisions which have been made and their results. We see life as God sees it, with only two divisions of humanity, the godly and the ungodly. We see the vanities and petty ambitions of men fade as a morning mist into nothingness before the realities of eternal salvation and damnation. The true meaning of life is made clear to us. We are permitted to look far into the future and see ourselves standing with the host of all nations, for we, too, are either on the right hand or at the left of the Lord. Tremendous yearnings for salvation flow through our hearts. We long to hear the words, "Come, ye blessed of my father, inherit the kingdom prepared for you from the foundation of the world."

Christ will come again. All Christendom believes this, for it is the teaching of God in His Word. In spite of the doubts and denials of those for whom the material thing is all and who believe that what heaven he will have must be enjoyed in this life, we know that Christ will come again as King and Lord and Judge. The date of His coming? This we do not know, for God has kept this to Himself. "As the lightning cometh out of the east, and shineth unto the west, so shall also the coming of the Son of man be," and great will be the surprise on earth when that day comes. The unbeliever lives as though he will live forever, and disconcerting indeed will be the advent of our Lord. He will come in such glory, in such majesty and magnificence that the kings of men must hide in shame, for He comes as God's own Son, as true God Himself, to conclude the affairs on earth. He comes that He may claim His own and treasure them with Him in His glory, that He may separate the dross and cast it from Him. Awful in its scope is the work of Christ as Judge.

When the Lord comes, He will divide all mankind, the quick and the dead, into two groups. Not into castes or classes of intelligence, social achievement or wealth will He divide them, but into two groups—those who have followed His way, and those who have followed their own way. Gone all human distinctions and positions, men will on that day be known only as God's or Satan's, those who are sheep or those who are goats.

If we had only this text to guide us, we should surely conclude that the basis of God's judgment is human works and merit, that those who have a soft heart and show love and kindness to their fellow men in such degree that they make sacrifice to serve will surely be in heaven. In view of other parts of Scripture which tell us that Jesus is "the way, the truth and the life" and that no man cometh unto the Father but by Him, and, "Believe in the Lord Jesus Christ and thou shalt be saved," however, we know that the deeds of mercy by which we shall be judged must be the fruits

of hearts surrendered to Him in sincere repentance and earnest faith, for Jesus will then apply
His precept, "By their fruits ye shall know them."

There is but one way to heaven, one way to be
able to stand just and righteous before God, and
that is through the redemption of our Lord, the
Savior Jesus, who paid for us on the cross. Sin
must be removed through forgiveness, the wall
of partition must be broken down; other than
through Him there is no way. The attitude of
mercy and love and service to the brethren is the
mark, however, the badge of faith which is living
and saving. "Without faith it is impossible to
please him," but when imbued with true faith
one seeks to serve God by serving the brethren in
faith. So it is that the tree is judged by its fruit,
and the heart by its willingness to serve. Saving
faith is active faith, busy doing the will of God
by extending the hand of mercy and love to all
who are at hand.

Salvation is possible for all, for Jesus has done
all that is necessary for the salvation of the soul.
No one was left out of that great and wondrous
love which brought the King of kings to earth as
the little child of Bethlehem. No one was passed
by when all sins were paid for with the life blood
of God's own Son. Not only is every man included
in the atonement, but every sin of every man, so
that all can through Christ be numbered among
the sheep, all can look forward with confidence

to the time when he must stand before the Lord and hear his judgment pronounced. That so many are not saved is one of the great mysteries of all time, but the condemnation of the many who will be numbered among the goats must not be charged to Christ, for He has made it possible through His atoning sacrifice for all, even the most wicked and degraded, to come to Him and find pardon and cleansing, forgiveness, and right-eousness.

The basis for judgment is then the relation of the soul to Christ. "No man cometh unto the Father but by me," Jesus said, and made crystal clear how to be one of the sheep on His right hand when the great day comes. Those who have accept-ed Christ as Savior and who have been willing to follow the path which He has laid out before them, those who have been willing to see and confess their sinfulness and guilt and bow in deep humility to ask pardon and restoration will be the sheep.

It is God who determines how the sinner is to be saved, and He has given us but one way. Any other way, no matter how plausible, how intellec-tual, how reasonable, will not find an open door to heaven. There is but one way to be numbered among the sheep, and Christ has given it to us, "Whosoever believeth in him [Christ] should not perish, but have everlasting life." Those who stand on the right hand of the King do so because they have had living faith in Jesus; those who stand on the left hand, because they have not believed.

While on earth Jesus stood with arms outstretched to the ungodly, and those same loving arms have continued to reach out to gather in all the souls of men in warm embrace. The ungodly, the perverted, the unholy, the dishonest, the cruel, and the mean are all welcome if they would come as Jesus bids them. Many have refused to heed the invitation of the Lord, however, and in sorrow He was constrained to say, "Many are called, but few are chosen." Through the preaching of God's Word, through Sunday school and confirmation class, through printed word and the far-flung ether waves of radio the souls of men have been invited to hear the Lord and come to Him. Some have come; most have not. They have made their choice and they have refused to accept the plan of salvation the loving Savior has offered them. Men and women, boys and girls, wise, capable and learned, friends and neighbors, they have been invited through God's Word and have chosen to ignore the invitation or resist it. Christ has called, but their reply has been "too busy," "some other time," or simply "no."

These must hear the words of Christ, the great Judge and King, "Depart from me, ye cursed, into everlasting fire prepared for the devil and his angels." They must hear themselves sentenced to an eternity in hell, which, while labeled as nonexistent or at least in bad taste by our generation, is both real and fearful. Terrible words these, the most fearful that the human ear can hear, for they summon to an existence in the hereafter filled with pain and sorrow and bitterness and hatred, and worst of all, without one vestige of hope. There is nothing so horrible as the experience of hearing these words of Christ. It is a doom without appeal, and to it there is no end. These shall share the destiny of him whom they chose to follow in this life, and his dwelling place shall be theirs.

Not only the grossly wicked are numbered among the doomed. Among them will be many who by human standards are upright, honest, noble, and even great. By the world they are regarded not as sinners, but as good men and women. This goodness by human standards, this outward honesty and uprightness will not help them then, for they have rejected Jesus as their Savior from sin, and only Jesus and His righteousness can help them. They are doomed because they have turned away from Jesus.

A short time ago I was invited with others to visit a new synagogue. Since I was a pastor, the rabbi, a charming man, showed me through the building. He showed the scrolls of the books of Moses and the prophets, the Jewish flag with the star of David, the little sanctuary and the larger one, the choir loft, the office and the many assem-

bly and school rooms. It was all beautiful, out-
standingly so. There could be no question but that
these people were loyal worshippers of Jehovah.
But through the whole tour and for days afterwards a pall of gloom hung over me, for these
people, religious as they were, including the
friendly, conscientious rabbi, have not Christ.
They work and play and worship apart from the
saving grace of the Lord Jesus. How sad that we
cannot look forward to meeting these men and
women, so gracious and intelligent and charming,
among the sheep on Judgment Day!

How glorious it is to have a Savior! When it
stands in judgment, the soul needs a Savior. Those
who are numbered as sheep had an opportunity
to make a choice, also, and they chose to accept
Jesus as their Savior and to follow Him as Redeemer and Lord. Guided by the Holy Ghost they
realized that they were without worthiness, but
had sinned grievously against their god. In deep
humility they bowed before Him in repentance
and sought and found pardon and righteousness
in Christ. These will hear Christ's words, "Come,
ye blessed of my Father, inherit the kingdom prepared for you from the foundation of the world."

These are the most wonderful of all words,
sweeter than the sweetest music, bringing exulta-
tion and gladness. Far more wonderful than any
words which we can hear in this life will be the
words of Jesus to His loyal disciples who in faith

will be counted worthy to stand at His right hand among the sheep and hear His voice bid them enter eternal glory and rest. They will share the destiny of the Son of God in eternal peace in heaven, for they chose to be His and follow Him in this life. How wonderful it is to have a Savior, a Savior from sin, a Savior for heaven!

Inevitably comes the question, where do you stand? Are you numbered with the sheep on the right hand who will hear the beautiful words of blessing spoken to you, or do you belong with the goats on the left hand, who, having been invited to give yourself to the Savior, have rejected Him and have gone your own way in this life?

The way is still open to you. If you are not His, turn to Him at once. To put off the decision is dangerous. Becoming His means that, guided by the Holy Ghost, you must make a positive decision to give yourself to Him; you must repent of your sin, you must turn to Him, trust Him as your way to heaven. Then, and then only, will you be numbered among the sheep.

As in few places in Scripture the importance of actively serving Christ with the deeds of our lives is stressed here. The sheep on the right hand of Christ are sheep because they have shown by their deeds of mercy and love that in their hearts dwells the true and saving faith in the Lord Jesus. It is striking that no accusation of evil deeds is leveled against those who must hear the words,

"Depart from me, ye cursed!" They are not told that they are forever lost because they have lived such wicked lives, but because they have failed to show living faith in Christ by vigorous, active lives in the service of God. A lack of good works is evidence of lack of love and a lack of true faith in the Savior.

As faith captures the heart, it shows itself in love to one's fellow man. An earnest effort to serve coupled with confession of faith in Jesus is the mark of a heart which has been given to Christ. The selfishness of unwillingness to serve is a mark of unbelief. True Christianity abounds in good works, in deeds of love, of mercy and of self-sacrifice, for Christianity, as the tree of the parable, bears fruit. True Christianity is much more than "don't do this, or don't do that," for Christianity is not negative, but a force for all that is good. Too many feel that they are Christians when they refrain from the vices, but God would have it clear to all that, while His children do refrain from the vices, it is *doing* and not *refraining* which is the true test of saving faith.

Our lives must emphasize serving, doing good, activity for Christ. There are far too many "do-little" soldiers in the army of God. Not only does the Church and the cause of Christianity suffer, but a terrible question mark is placed over the sincerity of their confession of faith. Christianity lives. It is made evident by the helping hand extended to all in need; it is made especially clear by willingness to help men and women, boys and girls to become the sheep of Christ. Are you actively doing good works for the Lord? Are you ministering to the hungry, the thirsty, the stranger, the sick, the lonely, the imprisoned?

Here we face eternity in all its awful fury and also in its glory. We think of the horror of the words, "Depart from me, ye cursed, into everlasting fire prepared for the devil and his angels." We think of the eternity in which they must suffer fearful agony. Our thoughts turn to the many who could have been saved had they been willing, the many who could have been numbered among the sheep but who are now numbered among the lost, of whom we have known many in this life. Perhaps we number some of them among our friends, yea, even among our relatives. They have heard the Word of God, they were taught as children the salvation to be had in Jesus, they have heard the preaching of the gospel, they have received admonition from pastor and church member, but they have not heeded. Some time ago a young man sat with me in my office while I spoke to him about his soul and eternity. He told me that he was interested in what he could get out of this life. I pleaded and begged as best I knew how, but never a glimmer of interest in the life that is to come showed in his face. It is sad to think of the fate of such.

On the other hand, we think of the glory of Christ's words, "Come, ye blessed of my Father, inherit the kingdom prepared for you from the foundation of the world." Our hearts are filled with joy when we think of the happiness and beauty all who believe in Christ will enjoy. There are many who need us if they, too, are to enjoy the blessings of heaven. Will there be more souls to hear the words, "Come, ye blessed," because you and I have lived, and believed, and labored for the Lord?

You and I must also face this text for the sake of our own souls. Where will you and I be on that great day? Will we be with the goats who have rejected Jesus in the unbelief of indifference and neglect? Or will we be with the sheep who have accepted Him as God and Savior and who have witnessed our faith by earnestly living for Him?

God grant that all of us here today may hear the blessed words from the lips of Jesus, "Come, ye blessed of my Father, inherit the kingdom prepared for you from the foundation of the world." In Jesus' Name.

AMEN

TWENTY-SIXTH SUNDAY AFTER TRINITY

For the Father judgeth no man, but hath committed all judgment unto the Son: that all men should honor the Son, even as they honor the Father. He that honoreth not the Son honoreth not the Father which hath sent him. Verily, verily, I say unto you, He that heareth my word, and believeth on him that sent me, hath everlasting life, and shall not come into condemnation; but is passed from death unto life. Verily, verily, I say unto you, The hour is coming, and now is, when the dead shall hear the voice of the Son of God: and they that hear shall live. For as the Father hath life in himself; so hath he given to the Son to have life in himself; And hath given him authority to execute judgment also, because he is the Son of man. Marvel not at this: for the hour is coming, in the which all that are in the graves shall hear his voice, And shall come forth; they that have done good, unto the resurrection of life; and they that have done evil, unto the resurrection of damnation.

JOHN 5:22-29

Chapter Twenty-seven

Life's Basic Questions

THIS twenty-sixth Sunday after Trinity brings to a close our sacred or church year. Both the collect and the text for this day deal with life's two basic questions, the questions of life and judgment. What two questions could be more appropriate for the close of the sacred year? Has the Church with its festivals, its prayers, its teachings, preachings and admonishment from the Word of God brought us out of judgment into life? Has it given us that peace and assurance which joyfully proclaims, "I know in whom I have believed, and am persuaded that He is able to keep that which I have committed to Him against that day"? If we do not have this joyous assurance and peace I can assure you that no one is more distressed and disturbed about it than the Lord Himself who has declared, "It is not the will of your heavenly Father that one of the least of these shall perish." *For this cause* He came into the world.

I doubt if there is a soul among us to whom the
thoughts of life and judgment are foreign and
unimportant. Life and judgment pervade the
thinking, the planning, the aspirations and hopes
of all of us. These questions are the very woof and
warp of our day-by-day living. Consciously or
unconsciously, they pervade the lives of all of us.
In the midst of sorrows, defeats, and disappointments these questions occur with vivid reality.
In the midst of sin, cynicism, or even a boasted
indifference, these questions arise to disturb and
distress us. Undergirding and pervading our highest aspirations, our noblest ideals and our greatest
hopes are these questions of life and judgment.
Let us review some of these thoughts about life
and judgment which seem as universal as life
itself.

Some Aspirations and Thoughts on Life

The great variety of activities and plans in
which we engage give profound evidence of per-
sistent desires for a better, more enduring and
newer life. The mind is always in quest of new
achievements, new objects and newer satisfactions
than the present moment can provide. We are
filled with voracious desires for a variety of amusements of both the sensual and the intellectual
nature. There is an insatiable desire for the accu-
mulation of riches, there is a relentless drive for

a career of ambition in pursuit of honors and recognition. The business man builds his cash reserves for renovation and expansion, the professional man engages in research, the farmer increases his acreage and studies the new methods and machinery. There is a striking oneness between all people of all classes, and that oneness is seen in the striving for the larger and more enduring life. In the midst of all the aspiration and hopes of our earthly endeavors, we are seeking to resurrect the new and better life out of the old.

This is further evidenced within our spiritual lives. The desire for an existence which has no termination pervades the life of man. He is incurably religious. When a cynic indulges in a wish for annihilation after death it is not because nonexistence is in itself his basic desire, rather it is his choosing of the lesser of two evils. He would rather be blotted out of creation than to suffer the punishment for sin, and frank honesty forbids him to deny the justice and inevitability of punishment. Not annihilation but immortality is the profound yearning of the inner man. That yearning is cultivated and expanded in proportion to the rise of the soul to higher degrees of moral alertness, repentance and sanctification. It becomes the stimulus to actions that are noble, benevolent and Christian. It becomes the stimulus for sacrificial living and religious devotion. Whether we be indifferent or alert to things

Christian, a true examination of the soul reveals a strong desire for a life without termination.

Some Thoughts and Convictions on Judgment

We have founded many institutions and mediums for the exercise of judgment in life. There is a latent sense of judgment within every soul. In our dealings with one another and with the things of this life, we are constantly judging in one way or another. Our government is likewise engaged. We naturally separate the good from the bad, the moral from the immoral, the strong from the weak, the thief from the honest, and the criminal from the righteous. All the courts of the land are but places of judgment. We are convinced that our possessions, our virtues, and our very lives would be in peril unless we exercised judgment and punishment upon all evil. The sense of justice and the exercise of judgment pervade our daily living and thinking.

There is a pervading desire for a future time when all wrongs will be righted. There is something as deep as our own soul which says, "The day is coming when there is nothing covered that shall not be revealed, nothing hidden that shall not be made known." It is an instinct as strong as the instinct of immortality. It longs for a time when all wrongs will be righted, when retribution will fall on the transgressor, when there will be an equitable adjustment of human affairs which will vindicate the righteous. This sense of justice and judgment keeps saying, "Crime does not pay," "Honesty is the best policy," "Justice will ultimately prevail." Even within ourselves there is a desire for times of reckoning. There is a latent sense of justice and judgment in every soul.

Is man, then, more just or wise than his Maker? No, we know that what is true of justice here is true hereafter also, only to a more complete degree. God cannot be deceived. "Marvel not at this therefore: For the hour cometh in which all they that are in the tombs shall hear his voice and shall come forth; they that have done good, unto the resurrection of life; and they that have done evil unto the resurrection of judgment." We are all moving toward a last great tribunal, when every life shall pass under the final judgment of Christ. This we instinctively know and frank honesty forbids us deny its reality and justice. There is an instinct of conscience which answers the clear Word of God's revelation. What is that clear revelation of God's Word?

"They that have done good, unto the resurrection of life." The Giver of that life has declared, "I am come that ye might have life and have it more abundantly." The resurrected life has its origin in Christ and His love for the soul. It is the surrender of the soul to Him, the opening of the soul to Christ to come in to dwell and take possession. "It is no longer I that live, but Christ that liveth in me." It is the indwelling Christ permitted to take possession, to master, to mold, to exalt life here and to complete it in the fellowship of the saints throughout all eternity.

The resurrected life is within and of the soul. But that soul is a part of the fellowship of the saints which Christ has come to form, "Father, I pray that those whom thou hast given me may be one." It is a life, therefore, which loves the brethren. It looks out upon the world and sees the fields white unto the harvest and seeks to make disciples of all nations. It is a life, therefore, which ministers to humanity because it is ever mindful of Him who said, "As I lay down my life, even so ought ye to lay down your lives for the brethren." It sees sin and unbelief in the world and weeps with Him who said, "O Jerusalem, Jerusalem, how oft I would have gathered thee even as the hen gathereth her young, but ye would not." It is a life which is compassionate to need and remembers Him who said, "For I was an hungered, and ye gave me meat: I was athirst, and ye gave me drink: I was a stranger, and ye took me in: naked, and ye clothed me: I was sick and ye visited me: I was in prison and ye came unto me." It is a life, therefore, that is mastered and molded by the love of the indwelling Christ.

The risen life is the life which exalts and consecrates the things of life. It has money and possessions but handles them as stewards of His gifts.

It has talents but consecrates them unto His service. It has homes but seeks to make those homes the dwelling place of the indwelling Christ. It has offices, businesses, and farms but it says, "Christ runs my business."

"They that have done good, unto the resurrection of life." That life has risen because it has done good. But it has done good not of its own power or desire. It says, "Without Thee I can do nothing." It says: "It is no longer I that live, but Christ that liveth in me." "Thou art the vine and I am the branch and apart from Thee I can do nothing." "Thou must work Thy works within me."

The resurrected life begins here and continues throughout all eternity. "For we are persuaded that neither life, nor death, nor principalities, nor powers, nor things present, nor things to come shall separate us from the love of God which is in Christ Jesus, our Lord." "Because he lives we too shall live." Christ in us, "we have the victory which overcometh the world, even our faith." "For the hour cometh, in which all they that are in the tombs shall hear his voice and shall come forth; they that have done good unto the resurrection of life." "Thanks be to God who giveth us the victory through our Lord Jesus Christ." Have you that life? Let me remind you again of the profound desire and love of Jesus who said, "For God so loved the world that he gave his only begotten Son that whosoever believeth on him may not perish but have everlasting life."

The second clear revelation of God's Word is that there will be a resurrection unto judgment. "And they that have done evil, unto the resurrection of judgment." What is that judgment?

It is a judgment by Jesus Christ Himself. Our text says, "The Father gave him authority to exercise judgment, because he is the Son of man." The author of Hebrews says that Jesus is qualified to become our High Priest because He suffered and was tempted. For that same reason He is qualified to be our Judge. We shall, therefore, be judged by a man—not by an angel who never visited the earth. We shall be judged by the Son of man who suffered and triumphed and sorrowed and died. We shall be judged by One who will look into our eyes and read our souls with His own eyes, the eyes of One who was tempted in all points like as we are, yet without sin. For that reason it will be a judgment based on wisdom and justice.

It will be a judgment based on love. But let us not mistake this love for a soft sentimentality. Many a person thinks that because Jesus is our Brother and Savior His judgment will be watered down and we will be let off more easily than if left to the judgment of the God of Law. This will be no easy judgment. Why? Because our Brother and Savior has summarized the law thus, "Thou shalt love the Lord thy God with all thy heart, and

with all thy mind, and with all thy strength."
This will be no easy judgment. Why? Because
there is no tribunal quite so just as the tribunal
of love. There is no law quite so inclusive as the
law of love. Nothing quite so condemns as the
realization that we have sinned against love, a
love so wonderful as to proclaim, "For God so
loved the world that he gave his only begotten
Son." Yes, there will be a judgment. Our heart
tells us so, and the clear revelation of God's Word
is, "They that have done evil unto the resurrection of judgment."

Judgment and life, which is ours? I must not
close without recalling the good news. We read
in our text, "He that heareth my word, and believeth on him that sent me, hath everlasting life,
and shall not come into judgment; but is passed
from death unto life." Again in Romans we read,
"There is therefore now no condemnation to
them which are in Christ Jesus." What does that
mean? It means that we may pass from judgment
into life. It means that we may have it all behind
us. We may get it over now, this morning, if we
will believe on Jesus Christ and commit ourselves
to Him who is the Savior from sin. Does that mean
that we shall give no account? Is the word of Paul
incorrect which says, "Every man must stand before the judgment seat of God"? No, that word is
true. But we shall have to give an account of our
stewardship, not of our sins. The account for sin

is settled the moment we believe on Jesus. We are then justified, redeemed and have escaped the judgment.

This morning at the close of this church year, may I offer you this great gift in Christ? Even now, this moment, we may pass out of judgment into life. Even now we may have that new life in Christ and that power by which we are molded and mastered and by which we mold and exalt life. As Paul says, "Like as Christ was raised up from the dead by the glory of the Father, even so we also should walk in the newness of life." His is the kind of life we should live. His is the kind of life we can live, and we can live it because He lives to enable us to live it. I dare say that in our better moments—moments when we are our real selves, moments when we are unfettered by our lusts, selfishness, and self-centered ambition—I dare say that we desire nothing quite so profoundly as to have and live that resurrected life. Let us be honest with ourselves, accept Him as our Savior, and seek in Him that miracle of rebirth whereby we can come into the newness of life. What a joy that would be to the Lover of our souls. What a peace and satisfaction that would be to ourselves. What a blessing it would be to our fellow men. *For this cause* He lives and loves throughout all eternity.

O Master, let me walk with Thee
In lowly paths of service free;

Tell me Thy secret, help me bear
The strain of toil, the fret of care.

Help me the slow of heart to move
By some clear, winning word of love;
Teach me the wayward feet to stay;
And guide them in the homeward way.

In hope that sends a shining ray,
Far down the future's broad'ning way,
In peace that only Thou canst give,
With Thee, O Master, let me live.

W. GLADDEN

AMEN